Plantation Life and Beyond

Adventures of a Boy Scout, Swimmer, Soldier, Coach, and Boy Scout Leader

To Jo-Alyce

Plantation Life and Beyond

Adventures of a Boy Scout, Swimmer, Soldier, Coach, and Boy Scout Leader

Aloha & Mahalo! Spencer S. Shiraishi

Spencer Saichi Shiraishi

Kahului, Hawaii, USA

On the cover:

Spencer S. Shiraishi took this self-portrait with a camera he won as a competitive swimmer on the U.S. Armed Forces swim team in Europe.

A longtime Boy Scout, Spencer earned the rank of Eagle Scout and the Silver Beaver award.

ISBN 978-1456375072

Printed in the United States of America.

Foreword

I am honored to have the opportunity to write this forward for my good friend Spencer Shiraishi. I met Spencer through swimming, of course, as I did many of his Hawaiian clan. They were so entrenched in our early 20th-century swimming: great names like Coach Soichi Sakamoto, Bill Smith, Halo Hirose, Duke Kahanamoku, and so many others. Spencer does an excellent job of portraying the conditions they had to live with. Such hardships are difficult for us to imagine. The days of World War II were doubly hard on him and his family due to their heritage.

If you know Spencer, you know he is never without a smile and never just idling along. He is in high gear and always doing something for someone else, also mostly as a volunteer. Sixty years of volunteer coaching! I do not believe there is anyone in the history of swimming who has given so much of themselves as he has.

As you read the book and live through him the conditions that prevailed during his youth, you can see where he got his fortitude. He, in later life, used this persistence to gain facilities for the swimmers and to put Maui swimming on the map. I know how proud of Spencer Coach Sakamoto was.

During my visit with two of my swimmers, Arne Borgstrom and Greg Higginson, to the Sakamoto Invitational, we got to witness the results of so many hardships Spencer had overcome while leading the way for Maui swimming. The Coach Sakamoto Invitational was a sight to behold. The most memorable moment for me was when Coach Sakamoto himself was introduced and everyone put leis around his neck until he was consumed by them, and we could hardly see any of his face. What we could see had a marvelous grin on it.

Spencer has unbelievable recall. He tells us in so much detail about his childhood and all the people he shares his accomplishments with. He is so humble about the part he played in all of this. For example, the electronic timer and scoreboard chief he finagled through Colorado Timing—to have such modernized technical equipment there on Maui at that early date—not to mention the pools he helped instigate.

The swimming on Maui has a great and lasting tradition due so much to the one and only Spencer Shiraishi. I believe that every swimmer, parent, or coach would profit by reading how one person can make such a difference. I know there are others like Spencer, but not many would equal his efforts. This in turn would motivate others to do more. His perseverance and stick-to-the job tactics need to be duplicated in many places.

The many people who have benefited from his personal volunteerism are uncountable. His contributions include so many things beyond swimming, such as the endless hours he spent doing Boy Scout work. He not only was an Eagle Scout, but led many others as well.

I've have heard it said more than once that when you have a job that needs doing, find the busiest person and give the job to him. This is a picture of Spencer up close.

I am glad and consider myself fortunate to know and count among my friends around the world Spencer Shiraishi. He has made my life brighter with his smile and friendship. He has made me wonder at a man who has given so much of himself. His wife, Wilma, whom he lost a few years back, was so much of all of this. With the raising of their family and the countless potlucks, one can see the teamwork they had to have enjoyed.

Bless you, Spencer, I know there is a place waiting for you in heaven and countless friends who will welcome you. Lots of love, my friend, you have made my life richer.

Coach Don Gambril

Former Head Swimming Coach at University of Alabama.
Men's National Team Coach -- 1989
Head Olympic Coach -- 1984 Los Angeles Olympic Games -- 21 gold medals
Olympic coach -- Los Angeles 1984; Moscow 1980; Montréal 1976; Munich 1972; Mexico City 1978
Coach -- 13 USA national teams; head coach 1983 Pan-American Games
International Swimming Hall of Fame -- inducted 1983

Foreword

I really didn't get to know my friend Spencer Saichi Shiraishi until he had been long retired from *The Maui News*. I knew of him from stories, like his tower-sitting adventure when he volunteered to spend five days and nights exposed on a tiny platform in the KMVI radio antenna tower raising money for the Community Chest. (He raised $6,000 and acquired a severe sunburn.) I knew he was Chief Engineer for Maui Pub's radio station and short-lived TV station and "troubleshooter" for the press, but I only became good friends with him when we found we had a mutual interest in the history of the company.

It started with a Mapuco flag. After the flagpoles were removed in front of the Quonset huts, the American and Hawaiian flags that had flown there went up the mountain to other poles at the KMVI site, but the company flag was given to Spencer. It was yellow and black (Maui colors) with MAUI NO KA OI in a circle around a quill pen crossed with a lightning bolt as symbols dividing "MPCo, KMVI and MAUI NEWS." A one-of-a-kind design. While housecleaning in 2003, Spencer found the flag had been put in a barrel in his garage after his wife had died. He felt it should "return home" and brought it to my office at *The Maui News*. It is still in good enough shape to have been flown above *The Maui News* float in last year's Maui County Fair parade.

From that beginning, we went on to years of reminiscences of the old days at the company and on Maui. Spencer has an amazing memory, a sense of humor, a fun kolohe streak, and a great deal of kindness. I interviewed Spencer for several *Maui News* employee newsletter articles about the adventurous old days with KMVI and the tower, about the flag, and for a profile, learning new things all the time. I think we only differ in opinion on Las Vegas; he enjoys frequent trips there as so many Island people do, whereas once was enough for me, when my husband and I stopped off on our honeymoon trip.

To my delight, Spencer started writing a memoir of his growing up in Nashiwa Camp, being a Boy Scout, and his experiences with swimming and in the Army. From a modest 30-page manuscript written in his unique style, the book grew to its present size, as more and more of his life needed to be included. I think it is a real gem of personal history and of Maui history. We are so fortunate that it is here, and we owe a great deal of gratitude to Spencer for sharing so much of his life.

Mary "Maizie" Cameron Sanford
Former publisher of *The Maui News*

Preface

Initially, the stories in this book were intended to be concentrated on my Boy Scout activities and the uncomplicated and freelance type of plantation living before, during and after World War II.

However, memories of my golden age and the pleasant past just kept pouring through my fingers on the computer: swimming against a world-class champion as a seventh grader, a first-time successful swimming coach as a ninth grader at Paia School, my exploits in the Army and introduction to racial bias on the mainland, swimming and adventures in Europe, successful interfaith and interracial marriage to a German Fräulein beauty (against the will of my mother), associations with the USA Olympic swimming head coaches, and my involvement as only survivor of the original four who formulated the age group swimming program on Maui.

Hence, this book contains a delicious plate of diverse experiences with the spice of humor and satisfying personal encounters.

Please enjoy a relaxing moment from your daily routine while leisurely reading the fruit-salad-type features in this book!

I would like to offer my tons of MAHALOs to Cecelia Romero, a teacher at Baldwin High School, Mary (Maizie) Sanford of *The Maui News* and Jill Engledow for their untarnished kokua in proofreading and editing the manuscript.

Spencer Saichi Shiraishi
Kahului, November 2010

Plantation Life

Maui boys in the Boy Scout uniform during World War II felt the war was not far away. They felt as if they were a part of the armed forces as they experienced numerous exciting exploits and provided rewarding services to our country, the United States of America. Other boys of their age missed out on the adventures Boy Scouts experienced, and they did not benefit from the lessons the Boy Scouts learned through those adventures and treasured, deep-rooted friendships.

The story of the Boy Scouts and reflections of growing up in the plantation camps on Maui are vivid, perhaps a little faded but not forgotten, memories dating back to the late 1930s, before the infamous attack on Pearl Harbor on the morning of Dec. 7, 1941, and during the days and years of World War II and after.

I became a member of the Boy Scouts of America about 1940, as a Tenderfoot Scout in Troop 10, sponsored by the Paia Congregational Church in Upper Paia. The church was located just across the once prosperous Nashiwa Bakery and Store. The Scoutmaster of Troop 10 was Mr. Sam Hironaka, an employee of the Maui Agricultural Company.

Before venturing into the services, experiences and contributions of the Boy Scouts and the youthful years of a plantation laborer's second son before, during and after World War II, a little background of growing up in the plantation camp and the character-building way of life of the writer should be explored.

We lived on Lanai for several years before settling on Maui. There was nothing to do on Lanai. As I recall, during my short years on Lanai there were a couple of swings and seesaws in the park located almost opposite the post office and close to the theater. There were no basketball courts and no gym. There were many Norfolk pines that I used to climb in attempts to catch birds.

The Lanai school was located upon a flat area above Lanai City. It was about a two-three mile walk up on a dirt incline, and after heavy rain, it was difficult to negotiate walking on the slippery road.

I remember a shishi (urination) class or lesson in the bathroom. There was a trough about 10 feet long and elevated about 18 inches which the boys would shishi into. Some of us were too short, so we had to tiptoe to shishi. After we went through doing our stuff, we were instructed how to shake off the excess liquid before withdrawing.

There was a dirt road close to our home that the pineapple trucks used to haul the harvested pineapples to the harbor to be shipped to the Dole Pineapple Company in Honolulu to be processed. The road was on a slight hill, and the trucks would chug up snail-like, because they were loaded with pineapple crates, and trucks way back then did not have the horsepower of today's high-powered trucks. The trucks also were not equipped with rear-view mirrors in those days.

When the trucks were unhurriedly struggling up the road, we would run after them to harvest our own pineapples from the trucks. One day, when I was a third grader, instead of attacking a truck from the rear, I ran on the side away from the driver and attempted to climb the truck. However, I slipped and fell, and the truck's rear tire ran over my left foot.

I don't know how or how soon my mother came to pick me up. Our home was about 50-100 yards from the scene of the accident. My mother could have heard me crying, or somebody could have told her about my mishap. My mother carried me about a mile to the Lanai General Hospital.

The bone on my foot was exposed, and the skin was dangling on the sides with blood dripping freely. I was hospitalized for about three months, and after 77 years I still have a scar on the left foot as a reminder of my blunder.

At the time of the accident, my mother was breast-feeding my sister, Jean. After my mother lugged me to the hospital, her milk stopped flowing. So my sister started drinking formula baby milk. My sister blames me (not maliciously) for her shortness in height, because I unintentionally deprived her of the full benefits of nutritious breast-feeding.

Nashiwa Store in Upper Paia.   Maui Historical Society photo

My adventures continued, luckily without injury, after we moved to Maui, where I became a member of Troop 10. The youngsters living in the plantation camps were very active and full of life and fun. Most of the members of Troop 10 were from Upper Paia, in a camp known as the Nashiwa Camp, because of the well-known landmark, Nashiwa Bakery and Store. There was a busy bus stop next to the Nashiwa Bakery. Two of Troop 10's members hailed from Lower Paia, where, today, is a growing and bustling community. Lower Paia, before, during and after World War II was a low-keyed and small snoozy town with a famous hamburger stand called Wimpy's on the right corner of Hana and Baldwin Avenues.

A private family, Mr. and Mrs. Mihara, operated a public bath facility (furo) for wahine (women) and kane (men) in Nashiwa Camp. The furos were made of concrete, about 5 feet wide, 8 feet long and 3 feet deep.

Boy, was it fun and comforting, to run semi-nude through the church grounds and between the homes after swimming in the cold water of the punawai (pond), and jump into the welcoming warm water at the furo. There was a puka (hole) about six inches by eight inches, between the kane and wahine furos, near the individual knobs to control the hot and cold water for each furo, and through the puka we could see the wahines walking back and forth. However, we were very innocent youngsters in those days, and we did not stare.

There was a concrete slab about 12 inches wide, 8 feet long, and about 18 inches high on the outside of the furo, where one would wash and rinse before entering the furo. On the inside was another same-sized concrete slab, where one could sit and talk stories. Across the slab, which was about 3 feet deep, one could sit for a soothing and relaxing moment with the warm water level up to the neck.

There was a cold shower in a corner, which was exposed through the puka from the wahine side of the furo. Since there were no toilet facilities, there was a small canal next to the concrete side wall where one could shishi (urinate), and the water from the furo and the shower would flow into the canal and out of the building.

In Nashiwa Camp, there was a miniature canal with a trickle of water that flowed constantly. This canal, about 6 inches wide and 8 inches deep, was between the rows of homes. Since there were no private bathrooms and toilets in the homes, usually men and boys would shishi in the canal. There was a wash basin, made of concrete, about 18 inches wide, 2 feet long and 8 inches deep, where people would wash their hands and feet before entering their homes, and that water would also journey into the canal.

The homes built by the plantation company were made of wood. I do not recall any homes being burnt down, although most of them were equipped with kerosene stoves. Our home had a spacious kitchen, two bedrooms with closets, a living room and a porch. My brother and I shared one bed and my three skinny sisters bedded together on a double bed in the same room with our parents. My sisters shared the same room with our parents until my brother and I went into the service.

There were five doors leading into the home, three on the elevated porch. One led into a closet and then into the bedroom, another into the living room and the third into the kitchen. On the other side of our

4

home was a screened door that led into a small storage room surrounded by screen to keep out insects and flies. From the small storage room, there was a door into the kitchen. Inside our home were three doorways, one from the kitchen into the boys' bedroom, another from the bedroom into the living room and one from the living room into the master bedroom. The only door that would close inside our home was between the living room and the master bedroom.

Our outside doors were never locked, way back then.

There was a single running faucet and a sink in our home for the seven of us to brush our teeth and wash our hands and faces. We had a lone mirror, about 14 by 20 inches, in our entire home to groom ourselves. It was in our bedroom, and I can picture my father, after coming home from the furo, putting a little hair cream in the palm of his left hand, rubbing his hands together and applying it on his hair. Our father's almost pure silvery hair sparkled like a diamond and made him look dignified and handsome.

After my homework and before going to sleep, I prepared a firewood stove outside the home every night. I would wash the rice and place the rice pot over the firewood stove. My mother would awake early in the morning, ignite the firewood to cook the rice and prepare lunch for our father to take to work.

Since we didn't have a refrigerator, we hardly had any leftovers. Whatever leftovers we had were kept in a screened container that was elevated about two feet from the floor. It was about 5 feet tall, 3 feet wide and 2 feet deep. The legs of this "refrigerator" were immersed in a small aluminum can with water to prevent ants and other insects from crawling up the legs and into the food.

A wooden building, about 8 feet square, housed the toilet facilities nestled between homes. The toilet houses were located between four homes along the rows and rows of homes, a great engineering achievement. It was shared by four families and divided by wooden walls for privacy. Each family's share of the toilet house consisted of two pukas, one small for children and a large one for the adults. At times, when people in the toilet house knew each other, they would socialize verbally between the walls while doing their business. Since there were no toilet tissues, or perhaps people were unaware of them, newspaper or whatever paper that was available was crumpled to make it

5

soft for usage. The average distance between the four homes and the shared toilet house was about 15 to 25 yards.

The depth of the toilet house was about 8 to 10 feet, and we could hear the thump whenever we deposited. Rats almost the size of a small mongoose roamed about. The rats flourished because the toilet house was in close proximity to the homes. Sometimes they would enter the attic in the home, and when they chased each other at nights, it sounded like rolling thunder and would scare my sisters. My father made a homemade trap and we were able to snare the huge rats by the numbers. We disposed of them in the toilet house after they were killed.

An unforgettable and stinky experience that occurred in the1940s will be shared with the readers of this book. This smelly episode was previously dispensed only among my three sisters, Alice, Jean and Jane and my son, Spencer Jr., his wife Ululani, grandchildren Riley, Spencer E.P. and Quinn…until now.

My father loved animals and took very good care of them, so naturally my love for animals also grew. We had chickens, rabbits and ducks. My father hand built the cages for the chickens and rabbits. The ducks were kept underneath the house, which was elevated about 3 to 4 feet. As a treat, I would bring home guppies from the ditch by the punawai and put them in a small pond about 2 feet square and 6 inches in depth for the ducks to enjoy.

Many times I would walk two or three miles toward and into the cane fields to gather two bags of milkweed for the rabbits, enough to last for about two to three weeks. At times I would borrow a bike from our neighbor's son, Tatsumi Imada, about three houses away, and bike to the cane fields to bring home three bags of milkweed. Unknowingly, I was doing the sugar company a huge favor by pulling milkweed among the sugar cane.

I used to play with a pet rabbit, with colors of brown and white and with a little splash of black in between, whenever I could. It was a comely looking rabbit. I trained the rabbit to stand for food, and it was good company.

One day, I took the rabbit into the toilet house and played for a while. We usually left the door of the toilet house open because of the strong offensive smell. After crumpling the paper and when I lifted my okole (butt) to clean, the rabbit jumped into the hole and went to the bottom with a loud thump. The rabbit must have initially thought that the dark hole was like going home.

My immediate thought was, "How can I get the rabbit out of the 'dungeon'?" I could hear the rabbit hopping occasionally and felt very guilty that I might not be able to save the rabbit. I lifted the toilet cover with the two pukas, but much to my dismay, I couldn't see a thing. There wasn't a thread of light. It was darker than dark. We didn't have any flashlight in those days. The fetidness was overwhelming.

I immediately looked for something that I could use to go down the dark hole to save the rabbit. I came across a hose and tied it, I believe to a water pipe, and dangled the other end into the dungeon and started my rescue mission. At first the stench was awful. I held my breath as long as I could and started to go down the hose. When I felt the bottom, with the feces about knee deep, I couldn't smell anything. The smell completely escaped my mind, perhaps because of my intense concentration in my desire to locate the rabbit. My only thought was to save the rabbit. It was so dark that I couldn't see a thing. Whenever I heard the rabbit hop, I would move in that direction languorously with my hands, scraping the top of the feces to find the rabbit. Finally, after seemed like ages at that time, I was able to grab the rabbit along with some feces. I placed the rabbit and the feces between my body and the shirt, and being positive that the buttons were secured, I sluggishly started to feel my way to the hose.

Up to today, the year of 2010, I still don't know how I was able to climb the hose into the fresh air, because my hands were slippery with feces. I told my grandchildren, jokingly, perhaps it was rabbit power or perhaps a divine intervention. Thinking back to that day, I could have suffocated and died by inhaling the gas that was trapped in the cesspool.

Today, when I see the TV series, "I Shouldn't Be Alive," it reminds me of the potentially fatal and nightmarish time I spent at the bottom of the whiffy cesspool.

Also, reminiscing back to that day, perhaps my upbringing as a Boy Scout played a key role in my desire to save the rabbit. At the Scout meetings, before we did anything, we always recited the Scout Oath: "On my honor, I will do my best to do my duty to God and my Country and to obey the Scout Law, to help other people at all times,

7

to keep myself physically strong, mentally awake and morally straight"; the Scout Motto, "Be Prepared"; the Scout Slogan, "Do a good turn daily" and the Scout Law, "A Scout is Trustworthy, Loyal, Helpful, Friendly, Courteous, Kind, Obedient, Cheerful, Thrifty, Brave, Clean and Reverent."

The phrase, "to help other people at all times" in the Scout Oath, could also be interpreted as "to help animals at all times." And the words "Helpful, Kind and Brave" from the Scout Law, could have been instilled within my soul from the Scout meetings to inspire me to go beyond the call of everyday life to rescue the rabbit.

In today's modern world, especially in the USA, perhaps the population cannot visualize the conditions that the people endured utilizing the four-family shared toilet houses. During World War II, at the now abandoned former US Army Air Force Base at the Puunene Airport, there were several small wooden structures with chimneys that looked like toilet houses along the Mokulele Highway. I never stopped to check whether they were toilets, but if they were, looking at the small size of the building, they were meant for individual usage. And with chimneys built into them, the occupant did not experience the extreme offensive odor that the plantation population tolerated.

The former Puunene Airport was the mainstream for military air strikes against the Japanese forces. The many B-17 Flying Fortress bombers stationed at the Puunene Airport were instrumental in hastening the termination of the world conflict. We could see them coming and going during the day-light hours and could hear them in the evenings. Nobody complained about the thundering noise created by the bombers and the fighter planes. It was sort of a peaceful and restful noise, knowing that we civilians were well protected.

There were two barbershops in Upper Paia. They were located in Store Camp. One was called the Hamamoto Barber Shop, located close to the store. The other was operated by the mother of my classmate and fellow Scout, Arthur Uyeda. The barber shop was located just makai of the Paia Congregational Church on Baldwin Avenue and diagonally across the Nashiwa Store.

As youngsters, we used to sing a song, as if we were advertising the barbershops. It went something like this: "Shave and a haircut, two bits, make the barber look sick."

8

Yes, in those days many years ago, a shave and a haircut were just 25 cents. I don't know how the barbers were making money on such a meager charge. During the summers, many of us kids would cut each other's hair with ordinary scissors and comb. We also used to cut our heads bald.

Maui Agricultural Company (MACo) built a softball field, a dirt basketball court with two backboards with baskets and a huge field to play football next to the Paia Hongwanji Church. With World War II in full swing, the company plowed the football field so that individual families could cultivate vegetables in Victory gardens. We carried water with buckets for about 75 to100 yards to irrigate the vegetables.

Paia train and bus station, left. The post office is under the arches at right.
Maui Historical Society photo.

The sugar company was very generous. It provided free housing, free electricity and free water and even delivered kiawe branches to use as fire wood so that the people could do their laundry with hot water. As far as the drinking water was concerned, it wasn't the high-quality type of drinking water we know today. At times, after a heavy rain, we would see brownish water. We used to attach an empty Bull Durham tobacco bag as a filter on the faucet to trap any foreign items.

9

Many times, the water would trickle out weakly from the faucet. We would remove the Durham bag, only to find whole dead guppies along with skeletons of guppies, stuck at the mouth of the faucet. And we were drinking the water as if it was nothing unusual. There were no complaints of anybody getting sick. People who were drinking that type of water are now in their 80s and 90s. Perhaps the natural calcium from the guppy skeletons was good for the health.

MACo provided employment to thousands from all ethnic groups at the mill and in the sugar cane field. During the summers, many students labored in the cane fields to supplement the meager income of their parents. The future of the youngsters in the plantation camps before World War II was destined to be following their parents' footprints into the mill, the cane fields, the pineapple cannery, or in the pineapple fields.

Maui Agricultural Company sponsored a swimming team that trained in the punawai, and one of the executives became a Scout leader. MACo provided swim suits for all the swimmers. There were about 20 swimmers on the team, and we stenciled "MACo" on the front of the suits. Lester Hamai, a great backstroker, was the coach, assisted by my brother, Ikuzo. Lester had two brothers, Tiko and Patrick, who showed great promise before the war. Lester was the manager of the store that gave Store Camp its name. He later became the founder and owner of the Hamai Appliance Stores, with the slogan, "People you can trust," in Kahului and Lahaina. Before moving to Lower Paia, Lester and his wife lived behind our home in Nashiwa Camp.

On many weekends, my brother and I would walk several miles with our mother to the cane field where it had been burnt. After the cane field was burned clear of the bushy long leaves, a Filipino partner would cut the cane. Our mother would then stack the cane in bunches, and her partner would carry the sugarcane up a wooden plank. The wooden plank was about 10 feet long, 12 inches wide, and there were 2-inch wooden slabs about every 12 inches for traction while walking up the plank to put the cane into the cane cars. Our mother would also carry the cane in smaller bunches to put them into the cane cars. The cars measured approximately 5 feet, by 8 feet by 5 feet deep. They were paid by the number of cane cars they filled.

When we went with our mother, we would help her pile the cane in bunches, and my brother and I would carry them on our shoulders, a job called hapai-ko, up the plank and throw the cane into the cane cars. At times, we would carry the pile of cane 25 to 50 yards to the cane cars. The sugarcane was cut the previous day by our mother's partner, who did not work on weekends. The cane cars were railed in by mules on temporary rail tracks to the harvested area and pulled back to the main railroad track for the locomotives to deliver them to the mill. It was difficult work. We learned early by working side by side with our mother that hard work pays off, not only monetarily wise, but also in the kind of strength and endurance our mother demonstrated.

Harvesting sugar cane was hard work.

Prior to the practice of burning sugarcane before harvesting, the laborers used to cut the cane in its full greenery and brown long leaves. That made it extremely difficult for the workers. And as the story or rumor goes, a bunch of kids were playing with matches and accidentally burned an entire sugarcane field. After the sugar company had the burned sugarcane analyzed, and found out that the sugar content had not been altered, the company started to burn the sugarcane fields for easy access to the cane. For years we have seen the smoke from the burning cane rise into the atmosphere, with ashes falling in a wide area. People who were raised here since childhood became accustomed to the practice of cane burning. In the evenings, it is a beautiful sight to behold. However, today, there are many complaints about

11

the cane burning, citing it as a hazard to the health and for soiling the laundry that is exposed to the elements.

Today, there is no such thing as cutting the cane or hapai-ko or walking the planks. Everything is mechanized, and big trucks with wheels about five feet in diameter just roll onto the field. Huge cranes lift the sugarcane that was piled together by tractors into the trucks with ease, and away they go. That saved time and manpower, to the detriment of the plantation work force.

When the days of laboring in the cane fields were over for our mother, she started to do laundry for single Filipino workers. Every Sunday morning after church, I would load the clean laundry on a home-made wheelbarrow and walk three-four miles to deliver. On my way home, I would pick up the dirty laundry.

To support our father financially, our mother did laundry work for a part of the 4th Marine Division, between their combats in the Pacific. The Marines would bring the soiled laundry on a two-and-a-half ton truck with about six men, and drop it off in the yard. There were bags and bags of laundry. Our mother, at times, solicited help from another family because the volume of laundry was overwhelming. I don't know how our mother and sisters were able to keep track of every piece of clothing. Perhaps by the last four digits of their serial numbers stenciled on every item, like we did when we were in the service.

Our mother befriended the Marines and invited them into our home for refreshments whenever they came. Somehow, in between hand gestures and a little Pidgin English, they were able to get along. My sisters, who were in grade school, were an asset in entertaining them. The Marines were extremely friendly and kind to our mother, knowing full well that some of their comrades died in combat at the hands of the Japanese soldiers. They did not show any signs of anger and hostility, nor speak in any manner that would upset our mother. They showed respect and displayed plain ol' American good nature/congeniality.

Some were officers, as recalled by my sister, Jean Umeno Yamamoto, who now lives in Honolulu. They were Captain Baker and Lieutenant Cross and Sergeant Covelle. They accompanied the men when the laundry was delivered. The officers, especially Captain Baker, captured the hearts of our mother and my sisters with gracious-

12

ness and gentleness. We believe he came from Missouri, but he spoke fairly good Japanese, which kind of entertained my mother.

My visits with the Marines were few and far between, because I kept coming and going. Perhaps I mingled with them about two or three times. They were aware that I was an Eagle Scout because there was a poster on the wall near the door that read: "AN EAGLE SCOUT LIVES HERE." The posters were given to all Eagle Scouts.

Our mother worked and worked and worked diligently doing the laundry. Her working hours of ironing the shirts and trousers to military specifications extended beyond 2 a.m. every night. She then had to wake very early to prepare lunch and breakfast for our father and us kids.

Our mother would boil the laundry in a huge container, and with a stick would churn the laundry continuously like a washing machine. She would then transfer the hot clothes with the stick into a wash tub and scrub the clothes on a ridged wash board. After rinsing, she would hang them on the wires in front of our home, and our yard resembled something like a scarecrow clothing factory. There were no clothes driers or washing machines in those days. Even if they were available, we couldn't afford them anyway.

Our mother, like many other devoted mothers, sacrificed personal pleasures and items for the benefit of her children. Our mother passed away at the young age of fifty-seven without ever visiting her home country of Japan, which she had left to come to Hawaii and marry our father.

On many occasions, our father would visit his Filipino friends in the Filipino Camp after work to socialize, bet on chicken fights, roll the dice and drink. Our father was extremely sociable, smiling and friendly whenever he felt a little high. When sober, he was a good provider, a hard worker and a pleasant father to be around with. But sometimes he would come home a little too high, and he would say that he was going to commit hara-kiri, (commit suicide by inserting a knife into his stomach). So, whenever we saw him come staggering home, we would hide the kitchen knives.

Usually, the extreme drinking with his Filipino friends occurred on Friday after work. One evening, when our father came home, he was really, really drunk and kept demanding where the knives were. Our mother repeatedly said she didn't know. Our father became belligerent and in a slurred voice kept on saying, "You are lying, you are lying." Our father then grabbed our mother's long hair and started to drag her in the kitchen and into the living room. Our mother was crying and begging him to stop. Our father kept on dragging our mother around the living room. (It is rather difficult for me to continue writing this portion of the story . . . but will proceed.) I couldn't stand our mother crying and pleading with him to stop. I went into the living room and tried to pull them apart. Our father continued to hang on to our mother's hair. I then struck our father on the chin, and he fell unconscious. Immediately, our mother grabbed my hair and forced me to the floor on my hands and knees and ordered me to apologize. In a flash in my mind, at that moment, I wondered why in the world would our mother force me on my hands and knees to apologize to her husband after the painful ordeal she was going through.

I apologized . . . even though our father couldn't hear me.

My mother and I half lifted and dragged him onto the bed.

Our mother must have truly loved our father—and no matter what —stood by her husband. My admiration and love for our mother increased a thousand-fold after that.

The next morning at the breakfast table, our father kept rubbing his chin and said that it was hurting. Our father didn't remember anything about his uncharacteristic behavior the previous night. We told him what had happened. He stopped drinking for about six months. But, gradually he started the cycle of visiting his good Filipino friends once again.

After what had happened, I told my sisters that when I got married, I would never treat my wife that way. Candidly, I have kept my word, and with that burning memory in my mind, I faithfully loved and respected my wife for 50 years . . .until her entry into heaven.

Because of that incident, up to today, I have kept my distance from alcohol. I may sip a glass of red wine occasionally, just to put me to sleep.

Even while in the Army, I shied away from alcohol. Many a time, some of my buddies would encourage me to go with them to the bar in the barracks compound during the weekends. They fully knew that I didn't indulge in drinking alcohol. They wanted me to accompany them for the sole purpose of escorting them back to the barracks when they were too drunk to walk straight.

I remember a minor request for financial aid from my mother when I was stationed in Germany. My two sisters were planning to attend the junior prom at Maui High School and my mother wrote indicating that the family did not have enough money to purchase two junior prom dresses. Perhaps my sisters forgot or were unaware that I sent our mother $50 from my miniature buck-private pay. At that time, the request was an almost insurmountable gesture for me to fulfill. But like a good soldier-brother, I cheerfully sacrificed my pleasures for the sake of my sisters' happiness. I hope they enjoyed dancing in their pretty prom dresses. Perhaps the boys were fighting over them. And if they did, I know one for sure, Eugene Yamamoto, who later became my brother-in-law.

My brother was a visionary person during his years at Maui High School. I recall several arguments between my brother and our father. My father would tell my brother, "You must always obey your bosses (haoles)." My brother countered every time, saying that he did not want to become a laborer like our father. He said, "Look at you, you come home with dirty clothes every day and cheap pay, while the boss, with his hands folded, goes home with clean clothes, and earns more than five times your pay. I want to be like the boss." Boy, that's mighty big talk coming from a son of a common hard-working planta-tion worker. My father would turn to me and say, "Saichi, don't be like your brother, Ikuzo, you must obey the bosses." Our father's thinking habit was work, work and more hard work without any argu-ments, and obey the bosses.

After returning from World War II, my brother went back to his old job at CCC (Civilian Conservation Corps) headquarters in Honolulu. When he came back to Maui for a short visit, he confided in me that he didn't enjoy his work because people were telling him what to do. So, upon his return to Honolulu, he enrolled in a business college to sharpen his shorthand skills. Then he became a court stenographer. After a while, he became unhappy because the lawyers and the judges were telling him what to do.

With his GI Bill of Rights, he enrolled at the John Marshall School of Law in Chicago. The school was named after a former Supreme

Court Chief Justice, John Marshall. While attending school, he married a lovely wahine from Kauai and had a son. He graduated with top honors and returned to the Islands and went to Kauai to live, because his wife was born and raised there.

My brother's vision to become the boss was beginning to take shape. Upon his successful law exam, he was appointed as a judge on Kauai, under the former Gov. Bill Quinn. Now he WAS the boss. He opened his own successful law practice. At age 88, he is now happily retired with his wife, Fumi. Their son, Sherman, took over his law practice.

Our father, upon his retirement from MACo as a common field laborer and after attending citizenship classes, became a proud citizen of the United States of America, pledging allegiance to his adopted country in the old Wailuku Courthouse. Our father brought home a certificate confirming that he was an American citizen and a miniature American flag on a skinny staff that he placed on top of our lone mirror. We were happy with pride that he went on his own initiative to the extreme of becoming an American citizen at his late age of about 70.

The varied camps in the MACo complex system had names such as Filipino Camp, Nashiwa Camp, Mill Camp, Spanish Camp, Portuguese Camp, Orpheum Camp, School Camp, Store Camp, Skill Camp and maybe others that skip my aging mind.

Upper Paia and all the ethnic camps are now a distant memory. Yes, faded fond memories of care-free fun days and years throughout the plantation camps are now plowed under the cane fields. Friendships flourished among the many ethnic camps. A wonderful friend named Pompilo Bascar, from the Filipino Camp, came to my home every morning and, we walked together to Paia School. I used to hang around and go places with a Korean friend, Stephen Yang. My mother persuaded me at times not to play with him. I asked my mother, "Why?" She would say, with a smile, "Because he (Stephen) makes you look short." Stephen was about 6 feet tall and I was about 5 feet 2 inches.

Stephen had two brothers, Albert, mentioned in another part of the story, and Gus. I believe they lived with their single-parent father about eight houses away. A wonderful family.

Many of the youngsters in Nashiwa Camp inherited nicknames, such as Midnight, Chocolate, Flower, Tin Can, Sidy, Cheakadee, Bulky, Booker-T, Lanky and others. It was a close-knit community, and crime was unheard of.

We went fishing one day with several friends and there was a fella who was about three years younger than me. When he tried to swing his line into the water, the hook accidentally got hooked on his eyelid. After that fishing day, he was nicknamed "Fish in the eye" forever. I cannot recall his first name, but his last name was Shimabuku or Shimabukuro. He lived one house away from me.

In another unusual humorous nickname-giving experience, a friend was dancing around a beehive behind a neighbor's yard. He was prancing like the Indians before going on a war path, like in the movies. Instead of an Indian-style war whoop, he kept repeating, "Make honey, make honey, make honey..." So, he was called, obviously and appropriately, "Make Honey" forever. His name was David Okamoto, and he lived about four houses away. "Make Honey" was a gifted baseball catcher for one of the teams from East Maui. He was not afraid. He would stand in a semi-crouch behind the batter, very close to the bat, and instead of giving hand signals, he would yell instructions to the pitcher to intimidate the batter.

We engaged in basketball and softball games between the camps and barefoot football competitions with authentic tackling without helmet or shoulder pads, angled for gold fishes in the punawai, and yes, swam among dead dogs, cats and chickens in the pilau (dirty) water of the punawai. There was a ditch that streamed through two camps and the people discarded their dead items into the ditch that eventually emptied into the punawai. Many times, the H_2O in the punawai had the appearance of a dark chocolate milkshake, so that we could barely see our hands in front of our faces.

Swimmers often drink water accidentally while training or just swimming. We were no exception, in that we occasionally drank the pilau water or dog soup, cat soup, or chicken soup water while swimming or horse playing or playing tag. We all survived.

The water in the punawai was flushed by gravity through a 3-foot-diameter pipe about two miles long underground. It went through two camps to the sugar mill to wash the sugarcane that was brought in by rail cars before being processed. There was a wooden housing around the 3-foot pipe to keep swimmers away from the potential danger of being sucked into the pipe. However, due to age, some of the 2-by-4 wooden protectors rotted away, and we would sneak through the tiny openings to swim in the small area as a challenge and to defy the hazard. We knew about the consequences but felt safe because there was a control valve about 2 feet in diameter and secured with chain and lock at the bottom of the punawai. Also, swimmers would climb onto the roof of the housing to dive into the murky water. Someone even installed a wooden plank about 6 feet long as a diving board. Ah, yes, it was fun, exciting and interesting. It had traces of the adventures of Huckleberry Finn and Tom Sawyer in books and movies. Surprisingly, there wasn't a single fatality or injury at the punawai.

We found other ways to have fun and get into mischief as well.

There was a ditch about a mile mauka of Kaheka Camp lined with concrete. It was about 4 feet wide and 3 feet deep. It was located in no man's land in the cane field. The water was cold and clear as crystal and came from a well located in a valley called Pump Camp. The moss at the bottom of the ditch was usually 1-2 inches thick and slippery, and we would slide about 50 yards down the ditch in the nude. There were side exits about 3 feet away from the main ditch with a wooden control panel that the workers would open to irrigate the sugar cane. We would slide into one of the side exits that was closed and run back to repeat our slides over and over again. Our yells and shouts of pure joy and fun could never be heard because there were no homes or people to complain.

As if we had nothing creative to do, many a time we walked through the Filipino Camp, just makai of the punawai to the rail tracks two-three miles away. There were rail tracks built on a slight incline leading to the Keahua and Pulehu Camps. We would gather grease that came off the wheels of the locomotives and the cane cars along the tracks. We would then apply a heavy dose of grease about 30 yards long on both tracks.

When we could see the smoke and hear the locomotive approaching from the mill with the empty cane cars, we would hide in the cane field about 25 yards away. There was a dirt road between the train tracks and the came field where we were hiding. We would stare between the long green leaves of the cane stalks at the locomotive and enjoy looking at the struggling train. We knew that our kolohe (rascal) undertaking was successful, because we did see the locomotive slow down and hear puffing at a faster rate and much louder when it came in contact with the greased tracks.

I hope the conductor, if he is still present in our world, would now know why his locomotive struggled for a short spell of time, that there was nothing wrong with his locomotive, and would forgive our youthful pranks.

There was sugar cane all around us, and we were able to chew on the cane for the sweet-tasting liquid at will. We would use our teeth to remove the husk and bite into the white flesh. However, there was no excitement in that. For thrills, we would hide in the cane field and wait for the train to come. There was a bend close to the Filipino Camp, and the locomotive would slow down making the turn on its way to the mill. There was a brakeman on the cane cars about the center of the 50 or so cane cars filled with harvested cane.

As soon as the brakeman disappeared around the bend, we would rush out and run after the cane cars and pull the burnt cane away from the cars. At times we would hitch a ride on the cane cars and jump off on the straightaway. It was fun, exciting and challenging.

If the brakeman or one of us should ever fall between the cars or away from the track, there would be no way for the conductor to see what had happened. It was a dangerous job and a risky enjoyment.

An unheralded heroic deed performed by one of my uncles more than half a century ago has come to life as I draw on my recollections of visiting my grandmother in Kaheka Camp in the 1930s.

My uncle Kachitaro Takaki was not favored by my grandmother Takaki. His older brother, Masao, who graduated from Lahainaluna High School, was the honored one. Uncle Masao, on his graduation from Lahainaluna, was hired almost immediately by MACo as a field luna (supervisor). He owned a car, but his car remained in the garage about 99 percent of the time. I would sneak into the garage many times and sit on the driver's side behind the steering wheel and murmur like the engine and make believe that I was driving the car.

19

Uncle Kachitaro was an ordinary employee of MACo and came from Japan to live in Kaheka. He spoke a little broken English and lived with my grandmother for a short while.

I went to my grandmother's home quite frequently from Nashiwa Camp. I used to collect chicken eggs and help her in the garden. I would store the chicken eggs under the house, and there were dozens of eggs. The house was elevated about 10 feet on one side because the house was constructed on the hillside.

My grandfather was some kind of a luna himself, and he was tall for a Japanese, about 5 feet 10 inches. My grandfather's name of Takaki fitted him well, because the word Takaki translated into English means Tall Tree. He went to Japan to visit his relatives before World War II, and we never did see him again.

On a weekend day one summer, Uncle Kachitaro and a bunch of us boys went to a punawai two-three miles mauka of Kaheka Camp, called the Cement Pond. It was known as the Cement Pond because, unlike the other punawais, it was lined with concrete. And there were groves of guava trees growing on the makai side of the punawai. We all knew where the sweet guavas were. There was a single tree that produced delicious white guava fruit. That tree was usually raided first, and that poor guava tree was never able to have a ripe guava, because the one-third-ripe guavas were devoured before maturity.

It so happened on that day that the punawai was in the process of being drained clear of the water to remove the accumulated dirt. It was still partially full, and there were no signs posted to warn swimmers of any danger, but we swam far away from the 3-foot-diameter drainage pipe for safety.

While taking a break from swimming, sitting about halfway up the side, we noticed a swimmer who was swimming rather nicely. One of us said, "Look at him swim, I didn't know that he could swim so well."

Actually he was being drawn by the current towards the 3-foot pipe. Without saying a word, my uncle jumped to his feet and ran down the slopes of the punawai and drove directly over the drainage pipe, and with his diving force he was able to drag our friend onto the safety of the muddy shore.

That was some bold rescue, and I haven't seen anything like that up to the present.

At that time and place, as youngsters between the ages of seven and 12, we didn't place any significance on what my Uncle Kachitaro did. But as the life picture goes backwards, and the blurred life journey becomes clearer, I think my Uncle Kachitaro should have been awarded a civilian medal equivalent of the Congressional Medal of Honor!

The rescued youth's last name was Endo, and my uncle carried him all the way on his shoulders to his home.

I don't care what my grandmother thought of my Uncle Kachitaro. I felt proud that he was my mother's brave brother. Perhaps his valiant display of courage could have somehow etched into my life to influence my later years. I don't know where Uncle Kachitaro is now, but at this late date I sure would like to shake his hand and hug his body with the fearless heart.

The punawai where our swim team practiced was located next to the Paia Hongwanji Church (now relocated to Makawao and known as the Makawao Hongwanji Church). The Paia Hongwanji Church social hall porch was a favorite gathering place for the locals to talk stories, play with yoyos, play marbles, play cards, play harmonicas and the ukulele. The boys and girls of Nashiwa Camp learned to ride their skates and bikes on the pavements of the church, and for extra exercise climbed the trees that were located on the church grounds. In the social hall, there were many Boy Scout Court-of-Honor ceremonies, and imported Japanese movies were shown there. The social hall was also a focal point for the aged plantation workers and retirees to socialize.

Members of Troop 10 who came from Lower Paia and between usually walked about two miles to Upper Paia for meetings on Friday evenings. The meeting place before World War II was in the National Guard Armory, near the theater and the baseball field and below the gym.

Harold (Doc) Ohata and Richard Ikeda came from Lower Paia, and Samuel Tanimoto lived near the railroad station close to the former Paia Post Office, between Upper and Lower Paia. Other members of the then Troop 10 were (as memory would dictate) Akio Alva Saito,

21

his younger brother Jimmy the Cricket, Gordon Okazaki, Mitsuo Tanaka, Manju Yoshida, Rikio Saito and Spencer Shiraishi.

When World War II erupted on Dec. 7, 1941, all Scouting activities were suspended and all schools were closed for several weeks.

Martial law took over the governmental functions and a mandatory blackout was ordered throughout the islands. (Martial law was terminated on October 25, 1944, but curfew remained.)

All windows that could shed light that could be seen from the outside were covered with blankets or any kind of material that would block any light-giving source, or the lights were not switched on. Marshals from the plantation, in pairs (usually haoles), would walk the roads to police the camps after sundown to see that the population complied with the compulsory blackout order.

Activities after sundown were in capital letters: ZERO!

Because the National Guard was activated, we were not allowed to have our meetings at the Armory. So we moved into the nursery at the Paia Congregational Church. Initially, the enrollment at the nursery was practically empty due to the restrictions of martial law. The first Scout meetings were rather somber and subdued. We didn't know what to expect.

When the Japanese invaded the Philippine Islands, there were rumors that the workers in the Filipino Camp were sharpening their bolo knives. Right next to the Filipino Camp was Nashiwa Camp, composed of a majority of citizens of Japanese-American ancestry, and people worried that perhaps the bolo knives were being sharpened to take retaliation for the Japanese invading their home country. When the rumors first surfaced, it was scary, and we were uncertain of the outcome. Things were rather uncomfortable for a while. Everything turned out well. They were just rumors.

There was a Japanese language school below the regular public school. Many of the young Japanese American students attended the school for an hour after the regular English school. All the Japanese teachers who came from Japan, including the principal and his wife, were sent to internment camps on the Mainland. Even some of the fathers of our friends were relocated. The Japanese-speaking school was closed permanently.

22

Little-known and almost forgotten is the fact that a sort of concentration camp existed in Haiku, close to the present Haiku post office, on the Wailuku side. Many of the prominent local fluent-speaking Japanese were incarcerated in the camp almost immediately after Dec. 7, 1941. The camp was surrounded with double barbed wire fences about 10 feet high and guarded with lookout towers. The internees were housed in dormitories previously occupied by the pineapple workers.

The internees were later shipped to Sand Island on Oahu and subsequently sent to New Mexico. They remained in the concentration camp in New Mexico until the cessation of World War II in 1945.

As we are all aware, there wasn't a single act of sabotage by the Japanese Americans living on Maui.

In the early stages of the war, we were discouraged from speaking Japanese in public. We were also encouraged (not forced) to change our Japanese names to English names. Hence, my Hollywood and British Royalty type name, Spencer. A good friend, with a true Filipino name of Pompilo Bascar (mentioned earlier), always calls me by my Japanese name, Saichi, whenever we meet, which is far in between. And I call him Pompilo; I like the name.

I think our Boy Scout Executive, Mr. Harold Stein, used his influence to persuade the military and home security authorities to utilize the Boy Scouts in some way. The Home Security Officer, man in charge, was Mr. Ezra J. Crane, the publisher and editor-in-chief of *The Maui News*. Mr. Stein and Mr. Crane were very close friends. Mr. Crane had a son, Charles, who was a Boy Scout.

More on Mr. Crane and Charles later.

The older members of Troop 10 received instructions to walk the roads after sundown to patrol the camps for possible violations of the no-fire-burning order after sundown. From the Paia Congregational Church we paired off, and in our uniforms walked the roads around the camps. We were assigned different camps. We instructed the people to douse the fires that were used to boil water for their baths and laundry after sundown, explaining that the fires were to be extinguished so that the enemy could not see any lights if they decided to attack at night. The people were really nice, friendly and obedient.

The Scouts in uniform also walked the camps, to collect newspaper and aluminum pots and pans for the war effort. We did not collect items every day. Periodically we would alternate what items to collect. All the newspaper and aluminum items were dropped off at the side entrance of the Paia Gym, facing Baldwin Avenue.

An unfortunate and unforgettable incident transpired to yours truly when I went to a family to obtain pots and pans. I will not target the camp, because people would recognize the ethnic location. I can clearly see in my mental picture, a hibiscus hedge and a dirt pathway leading to the entrance to the house. There were about three wooden steps and a wooden veranda with rails and a screen door. When I asked a lady if she had any aluminum pots or pans that she would like to donate to the war effort, I could hear her utter, "I don't want to donate nothing to a Jap Scout." After a few moments of silence, I could hear a male voice (perhaps her husband) calmly reassuring her that, "He is not a Jap Scout, he is an American Boy Scout."

After a while, the man patriotically brought out several pots and pans. I am thankful and proud that he recognized a genuine American Boy Scout.

The Scouts patrolled in pairs and went to the same camps every-day. We were able to meet the families and their pet dogs and they, in turn, were able to get familiar with us in our Boy Scout uniforms. It was a wonderful experience, except for that one incident. We felt proud that we could be a part of the war effort, to help the Red, White and Blue. We even received a patch that read, WAR SERVICE. And I still have it proudly sewn personally on my Scout uniform 'till today. We also felt that we were a part of the armed forces. We were honored and happy to wear the Boy Scout uniforms.

And for the love of my life, I cannot recall the name of my partner. Perhaps, if he reads this book, and remembers our days walking in the camps, he will call me and say, "Here I am." Please do!

The writers of the *Boy Scout Handbook* never did anticipate or foresee the type of experiences and services that the Scouts performed during the early stages of World War II. Nothing in the *Handbook* "prepared" the Scouts like the challenges and the unknowns they faced right after World War II began. Even though the *Handbook* neglected that phase of Scouting, the Maui County Council improvised whatever was deemed necessary at that time. The Scouts should have been given more credit for aiding our country when in time of need. Perhaps in the new edition of the *Boy Scout Handbook,* something should be added to describe the numerous ways the Boy Scouts in Hawaii, and perhaps on the Mainland, helped the welfare of our wonderful country.

I enjoyed congregating at the Paia Congregational Church in my youth. I was a member of the church choir, attended Christian Education classes faithfully, enjoyed fellowship with the Boy Scouts and participated in every church activity. Since I was going to church about four nights a week, my sisters thought that I was going to become a minister.

Classmate and friend Robert Matsushita and I were baptized by the Rev. Ted Schultz of the Paia Congregational Church before reporting for military duty in July of 1945.

There was a moment at the church that had a profound and positive impact in my life and taught me something that I try diligently to practice in my association with the youngsters at the swimming pool five days a week as a swimming coach. After a church function, about five of us were sitting on the concrete steps on the makai (ocean) side entrance of the church, chewing the fat. Two of my friends were smoking. They didn't seem to be regular smokers because they were taking puffs on a cigarette and coughing in between. Then, out of nowhere, like magic, our Reverend, I believe his name was Rev. Nishimura, was next to us. Instead of condemning the boys at the top of his lungs, he said gently and soothingly, "Some of you boys were smoking. You know who you are. I am not going to call the police or tell your parents. Smoking is bad for you."

And, just like magic, like the way he appeared to us, the minister faded away and disappeared in the dark. The way he talked, so calmly and reassuringly, it was almost like God conversing with us. The two boys stopped smoking overnight, and I try to emulate the manner in which the Reverend handled the situation in my everyday life.

All the roads in Nashiwa Camp and the other camps were unpaved. After heavy rains, there were numerous muddy potholes, and the company would fill the pukas with dirt. Many times the dirt contained lots of different-size nails. As a Scout, I used to walk the road in our neighborhood to pick up the nails and throw them away in the rubbish dump located about a mile above Nashiwa Camp. At times we would attempt to jump over the pukas, like playing hopscotch, and sometimes we would slip and fall into the muddy puddle and dirty our pants. If there was time before the school began, we would run home to change. Otherwise, we would go to school with muddy pants.

There were hardly any cars in those years. I only recall one man who had a car in our camp, a school teacher by the name of Mr. Kiyoshi Okamoto, about four houses away. He smoked a pipe, talked, walked, dressed and acted like a big shot.

School and War

In September of 1941, I was a ninth grader at Paia School, in Upper Paia. I was chosen to be a member of the FFA (Future Farmers of America) class, with about 25 kanes, no wahines. I was one of the FFA students who stayed at Paia School for this ninth-grade year. After graduating as eighth graders in 1941 in June, all the other classmates went directly to Maui High School as freshmen at H'poko (Hamakuapoko) in September.

Albert Yang and I were the school buglers. Every morning at a certain time, we would play "Call to Colors" from the balcony of the main building while the flag was hoisted and the students would stand at attention. I blew the bugle for two years. Albert, a brilliant student, became a private detective in Atlanta, Georgia.

The two-story main building housed the administrative personnel, classrooms, auditorium and the principal's office. All the graduation class pictures from years past were hung on the wall from the ground floor, up the spiral stairway to the top floor and to the auditorium. It was like a walking photo history of Paia School. The main building was gutted by fire some years past, intentionally or accidentally, and all the cherished and sentimental class photos went up in smoke with the entire building.

I clearly remember some of the faculty members at Paia School, like Mrs. Pacheco (third grade), Mrs. Tyau, Miss Kashiwa, Miss Wong, Mr. Kinoshita, Mr. Kobashigawa, Mr. Won and yes, our gra-

26

cious principal, Miss Mary Fleming. Miss Fleming always had a smile, even when she was scolding students.

Miss Fleming habitually wore something purple every day. She either had a purple hat, a purple scarf, a purple dress, a purple blouse, a purple skirt, a pair of purple gloves, a pair of purple shoes, or a combination of purple.

I remember a special tree planting ceremony on the Paia School campus one day. The entire student body gathered around a puka (hole). Miss Fleming shoveled the first dirt into the puka.

After the tree's roots were fully covered, Ethel Saito (Mrs. Winston Miyahira) recited a poem titled "Trees." If memory serves me right, it went something like this: "I think that I shall never see a poem lovely as a tree..."

Ethel recited the poem gracefully and went through the entire memorized poem without any hesitation and without any mistakes.

The tree was planted in the late 1930s and was located on the makai side about 50 yards from the cafeteria and to the right front of the main building, next to an existing monkey pod tree. The name of the blessed tree was jacaranda, and when in maturity, it would bloom with beautiful purple flowers, the favorite color of our beloved Miss Fleming.

Mr. Robello, the ageless school custodian, who lived in Kaheka Camp, diligently took good care of the tree as if the tree were his own child.

After more than 70 years, the jacaranda is still growing, and its majestic branches with the seasonal radiant purple flowers adorn the Paia School campus. And the spirit and memories of Miss Fleming keep on flowing whenever the appealing purple flowers grace the jacaranda tree.

I recall Mr. Kinoshita's hilarious advice to the young boys in the eighth grade. He said, "Look around you. All the wahines are neatly dressed and their hair combed neatly. They look beautiful. If you feel as if you would like to marry one of the wahines, do the following. Go to the girl's home early in the morning and knock on the door. If she

27

comes out and greets you, and if you still like the way she looks, then marry her."

Mr. Norman Ignacio, with the voice of a giant, was our instructor. Whenever he spoke, one could possibly hear his voice about three classes away. He also was a very humorous mentor, telling jokes in between his lessons. He was such a model teacher that my first ambition was to become an agricultural tutor.

I will never forget an outburst from Mr. Ignacio. During a class lesson, he made an off-the-cuff remark that, "Someday, man will land on the moon." Imagine, he said that way back in 1941. And with my big mouth, I said, "IMPOSSIBLE." He glared at me, pointed a finger, and growled, "It is impossible because people like you say 'impossible'." Wow, I'll never forget that! And the look on his face was beyond description. He was dead serious and positive about his prediction of, "Someday, man will land on the moon." After that heated exchange, the word impossible was erased from my vocabulary.

Years later, we Americans were the first to land on the moon. Mr. Ignacio, I don't know where you are now, but your words were perfect in predicting in 1941 that, "Someday, man will land on the moon." Congratulations!

I learned another important lesson from Mr. Ignacio. As a member of the Paia School ninth-grade basketball team, I learned the painful embarrassment and the sour product of negativism.

As we were walking to the cars before going on a basketball trip to Wailuku, I said jokingly that we were going to lose. Mr. Ignacio, our teacher and coach, must have heard my comment. We played in the old Wailuku gym against the freshman team from Baldwin High School. I was given the silent treatment by Mr. Ignacio, as I didn't play even a second in the entire game. Another teacher who helped to transport the team to the game asked me a humiliating question: "Why don't you play?"

Mr. Ignacio didn't have to say a single word as to why I didn't play. I fully understood why. I made a foolish and regrettable negative comment that could have had an impact on our performances on the court. It was like a self-taught textbook homework.

I don't know whether we won or lost, because my thoughts were on Mr. Ignacio's silent conduct of me in the gym.

I was not picked on the traveling squad for the entire season, except the last game. I don't know whether I played.

My expressed behavior before the trip may have triggered something in Mr. Ignacio's mind that could have reminded him of another previous similar incident.

I learned my lesson by the silent handling by Mr. Ignacio. No words or eye-to-eye contact were necessary for me to realize that negativism has no place in our classroom or on the field of sports or in our society.

Realizing the life-enhancing lesson that was imparted to me, I have mentioned the story of my negative assertion several times to our swimmers at the pool, that negativism has no place in competition and in life and should be avoided and replaced with a positive attitude.

Paia School, under Mr. Ignacio's guidance and the labor force of the FFA class, operated a farm behind the school, with about 50 egg-laying hens, a pig pen with about a dozen hogs, a pair of guinea hens and a vegetable garden. The pig pen was situated behind a pile of rocks, bordered on the other side with a fence and surrounded by paninis (cactus) and shrubs. Presumably, the rocks came from where the school buildings were constructed many, many years before. There were stone grave markers close by, shrouded with thick underbrush that made them virtually impossible to see.

I volunteered to take care of the farm over the weekends. I used to go to the school at about 6 a.m. to feed the animals. On Sunday mornings, I would pick up the garbage from the teachers' cottages on the school grounds to feed the pigs. There were two cottages along the south side of the school campus next to Baldwin Avenue and one above the school cafeteria, close to the tennis court.

On the historic and memorable Sunday morning of Dec. 7, 1941, I made my usual pick up of the garbage. When I came to Mr. Ignacio's cottage, he told me to go home because there was a war going on. War? It didn't register to me what he was talking about. I could hear the radio blasting away, but couldn't understand what was being said. I went about my routine of cooking the garbage for the pigs and feeding the poultry.

After servicing the pigs, chickens and guinea hens, I went home to get ready to go to church. I turned the radio on and heard the excited machine-gun voice of the announcer saying that the Japanese were bombing Pearl Harbor. It sure sounded like war, from the announcer's stirring voice. There were no TV stations way back then to broadcast what was happening. The only description that allowed us to imagine what was betiding Pearl Harbor was the announcer's dramatic picture words. It sounded like disaster was striking Pearl Harbor. And yet, on Maui, everything was calm and secure as if nothing was occurring.

I told my father that the Japanese were bombing Pearl Harbor and it sounded like war. My father's first reaction was, bakatari, or foolish —the Japanese were foolish to attack Pearl Harbor. It turned out that he was correct.

Even though the school sessions were closed for several weeks after the attack, I continued to go every day to the school to take care the farm. The door to the feed house was locked. But I felt that the urgency of feeding the animals was supreme, and somehow I managed to open the window to crawl in. Come to think of it, I don't know what happened to all the eggs that I collected.

Mr. Ignacio was a member of the National Guard, so he was called into active service. When he left, it was a sad moment for us. We did not see each other after he left. Mr. Ignacio passed my Boy Scout Agriculture merit badge. Thank you, Mr. Ignacio.

When school re-opened, it was nice to see friends again. The FFA members dug a trench behind the Intermediate class building for safety from potential air raids. It was 6 feet deep, 2 feet wide, and shaped like a letter L. There were steps on the short side of the L, where one would enter and walk on the elongated side of the L, about 25 yards.

We dug with picks and shovels and sledge hammers to pulverize the rocks. We did not have any gloves or safety goggles for protection. The FFA's sweat and aching-muscled-body-built trench was made between tall koa haole plants and rocks. After we were through with the trench, the sugar company came with mechanized diggers and made air raid shelter trenches in the school's playground for the safety of the pupils and the faculty. It would have been extremely difficult for the mechanized diggers to build a trench where we built, because of the thick vegetation of koa haole plants and the rocks.

There was another similar incident to Mr. Ignacio's surprising prediction of spaceflight in our sophomore year in 1943 in the biology class at Maui High School. Our teacher was Mrs. Buchanan, and she informed the class that, "Some day, we here in Hawaii will be able to see things on the same day and at the same time that the people in New York are witnessing." I thought at that time it was a really far-fetched thought. But I recalled how Mr. Ignacio lectured me in 1941, so I kept quiet. And what Mrs. Buchanan was referring to became a reality, in the form of what we know today and accept without any knowledge of the pioneering accomplishments: TELEVISION. Today, we are enjoying the harvest of the wonders of TV.

During our junior and senior years at Maui High, we attended school four days a week. Because of the shortage of labor due to eligible workers who had been drafted, every Friday, instead of going to school, the majority of the students labored in the cane fields to help the sugar plantation maintain production.

Others worked in the pineapple fields, as nurses aides, in the office and wherever help was needed. We also worked on Saturdays. The income was welcomed by the parents. All the hard-labored money that I earned went directly to my mother to help, in a small way, with the everyday livelihood of our family.

Because of blackout regulations, our Sophomore Social and Junior Prom were held on Sunday afternoons in the school gym. We always traveled by bus; they were running even in wartime, and there was no other means of transportation. We were all required to carry our gas masks, even while dancing. The only time that we held a school function away from the gym was our Senior Banquet in 1945, which was held at the Maui Grand Hotel in Wailuku. There is a gas station there now, where the majestic Maui Grand Hotel once stood. I don't believe we carried our gas masks at that time.

Our graduation ceremonies in June 1945 were held in the school gym on a weekend in the afternoon.

My Coaching Career Begins

In 1942, when the war was like half a world away, Mr. Teruo Tadaki, a faculty member of Paia School, asked yours truly to become the school swimming coach. Mr. Tadaki was the usual swimming coach, and I swam under him and for Paia School for three years. Due to the war, he said, his time was limited, so he asked me to become the swimming coach.

I did not know beans about coaching, but all the swimmers, except one, and I swam together in the punawai almost everyday. I accepted, and we trained in the punawai as best as we could. That was my first coaching experience, without any compensation, and ever since then, for more than 60 years, I have been involved as a volunteer swimming coach. There were no lanes and no place to practice our turns. The only place to practice our turns was at the wooden house by the pipe. We were unable to use our hands to turn because there was nothing to grab for the swimmers to turn. We were unable to practice any relay take-offs, and there was no place to position our feet for the start of the races.

We just swam and swam and swam without any technical knowledge support. Our only formal training in the various strokes was by observing the polished swimmers under Coach Sakamoto and trying to imitate their strokes. Imitation was our keyword. We didn't know anything about the flip turn. No stop watches to check whether we were improving. Perhaps we were the only school to train in a punawai with no stop watches. We trained in the pilau water among the dead animals as best as we could.

After our primitive style of training, we jammed into the cars of Mr. Tadaki and another faculty member to head to the championship site, the renowned Puunene Pool. Coach Soichi Sakamoto was a world-famous swimming coach at that time, and he used the Puunene Pool to train his national and world-class swimmers. All of our swimmers were rather intimidated to compete against his swimmers. Coach Sakamoto, a science teacher at Puunene School and the coach of that school, had never lost a competition in grade-school encounters.

So it was amazing that when Paia School won the final event, the 200-yard freestyle relay, Paia School became the champion over all the grade schools on Maui. This was the first time Puunene School ever lost, and it was the first championship for Paia School. We were elated. The winning combination in the championship 200 freestyle relay, as remembered by my aged mind, were Akira Tanaka, Tatsumi Imada, Jack Mihara and Hiroshi Nakasato.

When the championship was over, Coach Sakamoto came over to where our swimmers were seated by the shallow end of the pool and congratulated Mr. Tadaki as the coach of Paia School. Mr. Tadaki turned towards me and pointed at me and informed Coach Sakamoto, "I am not the coach, he is the coach."

Imagine, me, a first-time ninth-grader coach, defeating a legendary world-class coach and the almost invincible Puunene School. I didn't feel the impact then, as to what the boys from Nashiwa Camp accomplished. It was a monumental victory. For our giant-killing performance, we were treated to a tasty saimin lunch at the Hew Restaurant in Lower Paia.

Members of the victorious Paia School swim team from Nashiwa Camp were Akira Tanaka, Hiroshi Nakasato, Jack Mihara, Bobby Matsumoto, Tatsumi Imada, Roy Tsukuda and perhaps one or two more that escape my mind. Wallace Hirai was the only outsider; he came from Lower Paia. Wallace was our backstroker in the 150-yard medley relay team. Others on the medley team were Bobby Matsumoto, who swam the breaststroke and Hiroshi Nakasato, who anchored. I believe they came in first. In those days, there wasn't an event called the butterfly.

My brother, Ikuzo, wanted me to join the Three Year Swim Club (3YSC) under Coach Sakamoto to become a better swimmer. We knew that our parents couldn't afford twenty cents a day for the bus fare. So, he skipped eating his ten-cent lunch at Maui High School and I did the same at Paia School. With ten cents I would catch the bus, transfer at the Kahului bus terminal to Puunene's Camp 5 store and walk one-two miles to the pool. I would return home with the other ten cents. The bus terminal at Kahului was almost directly across the Bank of Hawaii building, which was formerly the First Hawaiian Bank office.

The first thing Coach Sakamoto corrected me on was my breathing. He said that my breathing was too high. Swimming in the calm water

33

of the pool at Puunene and the choppy water of the punawai were drastically different. While swimming in the punawai, we always lifted our face way above the waves, trying not to swallow the pilau water.

After about two-three months, my brother said that he got too hungry skipping lunch at school, and I told him the same thing. So we decided to forgo my swimming under Coach Sakamoto. Yes, asking twenty cents a day from our parents in those days were like extracting a tooth with no pain killer. Very painful.

While a seventh-grader at Paia School, I competed against Bill Smith and Bunmei "Bunny" Nakama. Bunmei was the younger brother of Keo Nakama, Coach Sakamoto's first National and World Champion. They were members of the world-class swimming coach Coach Sakamoto's 3YSC. Bill was attending Baldwin High School and already was a national champion and world record holder, and Bunmei was a student at Maui High and was also of national stature. Both Bill and Bunmei matriculated at Ohio State and became instant champions. Bill snapped NCAA, national and world records, and Bunmei was showing his stuff.

Our team, MACo Swim Club, competed with 3YSC regularly. At times we would swim at the Puunene Pool and other times at the Wailuku Pool. There was a bowling alley next to the Wailuku Pool, and we could see people crowd the windows to watch the swimming meet. There were bleachers, about 10 rows high, along the 25-yard pool and mango trees behind the bleachers. The bleachers were usually fully occupied. A huge board on the building listed the events and swimming records with names and times. The board was dominated by names of Bill Smith, Kiyoshi (Keo) Nakama, Takashi (Halo) Hirose, Jose Balmores, Benny Castor, Chieko Miyamoto, Fujiko Katsutani, Mitsuko Higuchi and Toyoko Tateyama.

Masaru (Pundy) Yokouchi is an established and highly respected name connected with the building of the Maui Arts & Cultural Center in Kahului. However, people hardly associate Pundy on his accomplishments in the competitive world of swimming. Pundy, with his height and talent, could have developed into a top performer for Coach Sakamoto. Pundy and I competed against each other several times in the 200-yard freestyle, and he always managed to beat me in close races at the Puunene Pool. Whenever the 200-free race was announced

34

for competitors, and while I walked on the mauka side of the pool to the starting end, I always saw Coach Sakamoto motion to Pundy, sitting on the makai side, to swim against me. Standing next to Pundy at the start of the race was like staring at Goliath, because he was head and shoulders taller than me.

Bill, Bunmei and I swam the 220-yard freestyle race at the Wailuku Pool. Nobody else wanted to compete against them. In the early years of swimming, there were events like the 220, 440 and 880. Presently, all the events are in even numbers, 200, 400 and 800. The 220-yard race required nine laps across the 25-yard pool, leaving an extra 5 yards at the end, so there was a rope across the pool at the 20-yard mark. Because the end of the race occurred 5 yards from the pool wall, there could be a slight human judgmental error of the times recorded. The stop watches were stopped whenever any part of the body would cross the rope, usually the finger tips. There were three stop watches per lane, and the median time of the three watches was the official time. However, if two watches displayed the same time, that was the official time.

I told the story of my swim against Bill and Bunmei only three times. Once on Bill's retirement party at the Pagoda Hotel, on Al Minn's retirement celebration at Kailua and to members of Maui Swim Club years ago. Bill retired as coach of the Kamehameha Swim Club and Al from the Aulea Swim Club.

What was significant about our competition? Perhaps nobody remembers that race, but I certainly do! Bill swam in lane one, I swam in lane two and Bunmei swam in lane three of a four-lane pool. I finished way behind Bill and Bunmei. After the swim, Bill, about 6 feet 3 inches tall, came over to my lane and lifted me up and said, "Nice going, kid." I shall never forget that feeling when he hoisted me. I could scarcely keep my face above the water because the pool was so deep. Also, I was short and still growing. If there were a photographer at the meet who took a picture of that scene, the photo could have been on the front pages of many newspapers. I don't know if Bill broke the 220 freestyle record. If he did, I would have been happy for him, because perhaps I pushed him to the limit!

Whenever I told that story, I always said I came in third. Never last! I never did attain the world-class status of swimmers like Bill and

Bunmei. But swimming against them as a youngster and placing third and being lifted by Bill after the race are memories I will cherish forever. That eventful race will be etched into my RAM (random access memory) until the flame of my life-guiding torch is finally extinguished, forever...in this world.

Bill attained the ultimate in his swimming career by capturing the 1948 Olympic 400-meter freestyle swimming event for new Olympic and world records in London, England. Bill was also a member of the victorious USA 800-meter freestyle relay quartet that erased the Olympic and world records. Bill anchored the relay team.

Bunmei later became the NCAA 1500-meter freestyle champion while attending Ohio State. He is a member of the Hawaiian Swimming Hall of Fame.

Bill Smith, along with teammates Keo Nakama and Fujiko Katsutani, and their legendary coach, Soichi Sakamoto, were inducted into the International Swimming Hall of Fame. Bill is now 86 years of age and Keo is going strong at 89. Both Fujiko and Coach Sakamoto have passed away and are now in the Swimming Hall of Heaven.

Boy Scout Days

Perhaps the final and the longest march by the Boy Scouts was the Maui County Annual Fair Parade in early October prior to December 7, 1941. All the marching units, including the colorful floats, National Guard, Army, different organizations and all the Boy Scouts gathered at Wells Park in Wailuku. We marched mauka (toward the mountain) on Kaua Street, next to the Iao School (which was formerly the National Guard Armory), turned right on Market Street, passed the old Wailuku Gym, the swimming pool and the former Boy Scout office and made a right 90-degree turn on Main Street and went down Kaahumanu Avenue. We marched the length of Kaahumanu Avenue and turned right on Puunene Avenue where Burger King is now located. We concluded our enjoyable march by making a left turn, where the McDonald's restaurant is now located, and into the Fairgrounds. I was the proud American flag bearer for Troop 10. Today, such lengthy marches are unheard of. The Fairgrounds in Kahului was the center of community activities for Maui County. All the high school football games, track meets, grade school sporting activities, horse racing, dog shows, boxing, etc., were witnessed at the Fairgrounds.

The Boy Scouts used to camp at the Fairgrounds for three nights during the four-day County Fair festivities. In those days, the schools were closed on Friday to allow the youngsters to attend the Fair. The Scouts pitched their tents and did their cooking along the left side of the main entrance from Puunene Avenue. The Scouts were utilized primarily as messengers between the fair office and the booths. Our job as Scouts included carrying money from the booths to the office.

During the early stages of World War II, the leadership at Boy Scout Troop 10 changed hands, and the program was not as stimulating as before. So, I transferred to Troop 30, sponsored by the Paia School. The Scoutmaster at that time was Mr. Clarence Yoshioka, a school teacher who subbed for Mr. Ignacio. My brother, Clinton Ikuzo, was a member of Troop 30 during his younger days and rose to the rank of Life Scout. On the weekends, to earn merit badges, I used to walk past Kaheka Camp, about a mile, from Nashiwa Camp, through the pasture and to Makawao, about four or five miles away, where Mr. Yoshioka lived.

To earn a merit badge in the 1940s, Scouts were required to seek a counselor on their own, with the blessing from the Scout Office. Today, there is a pool of merit badge counselors with different backgrounds and professions, where a Scout can make contact to earn merit badges. This makes it easier and more convenient for the Scouts to earn merit badges.

While I was a member of Troop 30, I had close friends at Maui High School who were not in the Scouting movement. After I talked to them about the benefits of Scouting, they became interested. They didn't want to become Scouts at such an old age, so I talked to Mr. Jim Ohta, who was second in command at the Boy Scout office, about forming a new troop. He was all in favor of the idea. We gathered five boys, but at that time, you needed at least six boys to form a troop, so Mr. Ohta suggested that we form a Lone Scout Patrol. That was fine with the boys. So, we called ourselves the Tribe Mohawk Patrol. The original five boys were Arthur Uyeda, Ernest Ishikawa, Raymond (Ajah) Nakasone, Edward Nishimura and Spencer Shiraishi. Instead of

37

the regular Boy Scout uniform, we designed our own T-shirt with "Tribe Mohawk" on the front and wore it with pride.

At that time, the former Boy Scout office was located on Market Street, about where the Romero Building is located, next to the First Hawaiian Bank. I remember Mrs. Ota as one of the secretaries. She was very pretty, helpful and friendly.

To be registered, we needed an adult leader. We asked Mr. Yasunobu Kesaji, a well-respected former Eagle Scout, to temporarily become our leader. He consented, but stayed just a while. Then I went to see Mr. Ray Gill, who was an important man with the MACo management staff, to become our head man. He became interested, and he was instrumental in obtaining an empty house, with one room and a closet, in Nashiwa Camp for our meeting place. I believe the house was utilized as a gathering place for socials by the Okinawan population in Nashiwa Camp before the war. Mr. Gill really got so involved with Tribe Mohawk that he wanted his sons to join our group. We went to his home in Lower Paia several times to camp in his yard.

Mr. Gill, a member of the so-called Maui Civil Defense, taught the members of Tribe Mohawk the Schaffer type of resuscitation and later the newer back-pressure arm-lift method to revive an unconscious person. These stone-age techniques are no longer practiced. Mr. Gill also taught us basic first aid.

We were having such a wonderful and an adventurous life that our membership started to grow. Our new additions included Lawrence Shishido, Harold Nako, Sakae (Saka) Uehara and others.

Since our membership grew, we had to change our name from Tribe Mohawk to Troop 45, an appropriate number because I would graduate from Maui High in 1945, and so would Arthur, Ernest and Ajah.

Somebody donated a wooden surfboard, about 15 to 20 feet long, 4 to 6 inches thick, that we could use in the punawai. Perhaps Troop 45 was the only troop in Maui County Council at that time to own a surfboard. It was so very, very heavy that it took four of us to carry it to the punawai. When there was a strong wind, the waves in the punawai would sometimes swell to about 12 inches high, enough for the beginners to enjoy the fun of standing on the surfboard.

Four of us, Arthur Uyeda, Ajah Nakasone, Ernest Ishikawa and I, went on a camping trip with Mr. Ohta in his car to Kipahulu one weekend. The road to Hana and eventually to Kipahulu looked more like a trail at that time, and it was bumpy with many, many pot holes. Some of us got so sick that Mr. Ohta had to stop. We camped in front of the one-room Kipahulu School. Mr. Ohta knew the area, so we followed him on a trail behind the school. We ended up on the beach where there were countless numbers of opihis on the rocks. There were so many opihis, and they were clustered together so that they looked like rocks by themselves. Mr. Ohta would take a rock and smash the hard shells of the opihis and, after washing the opihis clear of the shells in the ocean water, would eat them raw. We tried the same thing, but at first the taste of eating raw opihi did not agree with our system. However, by the time we reached the end of rocks, we were like veterans, eating raw opihi.

Also, there was a stream close by, and we would slide on the slippery rocks downstream in the nude. I was in the lead and, for some unknown reason, I stopped. We kept alternating walking on the side and sliding on the rocks in the stream. After a few steps, we could hear a loud roaring sound, like a waterfall. We turned back and put our clothes on and went back to the school. We told Mr. Ohta, and he said that we were heading straight into the ocean via the steam and the waterfall. Wow, we were lucky!

We had an active group. We once hiked from the end of the bus line in Lahaina, just about where the Lahaina Cannery Mall is now located, to Honolua, about 12 miles, with our backpacks full of food. We camped in the yard of Mr. Seki, who was sort of a supervisor for the Baldwin Packers Pineapple Company. Mr. Seki's home, surrounded by pine trees, was located about 25 yards from the Honolua Store.

In the morning, after breakfast, we trekked to Camp Maluhia, about 10 miles. Camped overnight at Camp Maluhia and walked to the bus stop in Waihee the following day, about three miles, for our trip back to Paia.

There were hardly any cars in those early days when we hiked from Lahaina to Honolua to Camp Maluhia to Waihee. I don't think we encountered a single vehicle, except the pineapple trucks.

39

We hiked to Camp Maluhia about every two months. It was like a second home to me. We hiked from the end of the bus line, either by Happy Valley or by the Waihee Store in Waihee, depending upon the bus schedule. We did not follow the road. Instead, we climbed a fence and went through the pasture, where we encountered several surprised cows. We ate plenty of guavas along the way.

We hiked from the end of the bus line at Lahaina to Fleming's Beach in Honolua on several occasions. We usually slept under the stars, leaving tents home to keep our backpacks light. The weather was very mild during the summers. There were groves and groves of Haden mango trees, planted by Baldwin Packers manager David T. Fleming, on the slopes just above Fleming's Beach. There were no temptations to go after the mangoes because we were Boy Scouts, and we respected Mr. Fleming's orchard. Fleming's Beach was a beautiful spot for camping and swimming and was kept in immaculate condition, with showers among the coconut trees. Now, the mango trees are gone and in their place are high-priced homes.

One day before I left for the service a fellow Eagle Scout and friend brought a crate of Haden mangoes to my home. There were 12 precious mangoes from the Fleming mango orchard, and they smelled and appeared so delicious, with colors of yellow, orange, red and a tiny streak of green. They were something out of this world.

That was my initial introduction into the wonderful world of the ono (delicious) Haden mango. If we had known that the mangoes in the orchard tasted so appetizing, perhaps, perhaps we could have bent the Scout Law.

The Eagle Scout's name was David Harada, perhaps a year younger than me. He was a member of Troop 5 of Lahaina. His parents owned a store called the Aloha Store on Front Street in Lahaina. As a youth I used to frequent the store on my trips to Lahaina, and his parents invited me to have meals with them behind the store several times. In fact, my wife and I also visited them when we first arrived on Maui.

David became a United Methodist minister and was elevated to superintendent of the Hawaii District of the church's Pacific and Southwest Annual Conference, with headquarters on the West Coast. I used to meet the Rev. David occasionally when he visited the United Methodist church next to Maui Publishing Co. The minister of that church had a son, Paul, who swam for Maui Swim Club years ago.

One weekend in 1944, David escorted several scouts from Troop 5 from Lahaina to camp at our meeting house in Nashiwa Camp. Before the sun settled behind the West Maui Mountains, we hiked towards Makawao and enjoyed a singing session at the Rainbow Park about a mile mauka of Nashiwa Camp. One of the songs that we repeatedly sang lingers in my mind; it went something like: "I'm forever blowing bubbles, pretty bubbles in the air... ." After the fun singing, we continued our trek toward Makawao and turned right just after passing Rainbow Park into a cane field dirt road. While hiking towards Nashiwa Camp at night from an elevation of about 1,000 feet, we were delighted and enjoyed a beautiful sight, the lights that illuminated Wailuku and Kahului. We passed the Cement Pond, passed Kaheka Camp and eventually arrived at our Scout Hall.

We camped on the grounds inside the historic and picturesque Lahaina Prison walls with members of Troop 5 of Lahaina, under the leadership of Ken (Soup) Nakata and Nobu Yabui. We also camped on the land next to the Baldwin Missionary Museum on Front Street, where there was a basketball court near by.

There were several Boy Scout Camporees at the now-revealed sacred grounds of the Malu-`ulu-o-Lele Park on Front Street in Lahaina. We even played football against Lahaina at the park, as members of the Paia championship team in the 105-pound barefoot football league. To learn now that the grounds are linked to Hawaii's royal monarchy, it makes one wonder at the abuses by which we have for so long demeaned the affable Hawaiians of the past who settled here ages ago.

We also ventured through Makawao, about four miles, to Kaupakulua School, about three miles. We did not have any tents, so we improvised a tent with branches for poles and intertwined grass between the branches for cover. We obtained permission from the Kaupakulua School principal, Mr. Norman Smith, to camp at the school grounds. Camped over night and traversed through the pineapple fields to Hookipa Park, about six miles. Swam in the ocean and enjoyed a restful day and night. On the third day, we struck out for Lower Paia, about two miles, and on to Upper Paia, about two miles, for home.

A bridge with rail tracks built on it spanned the Maliko Gulch on East Maui between Paia and Haiku. We tiptoed across the bridge to the other side of Maliko Gulch to climb the hill on the outskirts of the 4th Marine Division training site in Haiku. While crossing the bridge, we would intermittently listen for any sign of a train that was traveling our way, east or west, by gluing our ears on the train tracks. In case there was a locomotive coming, we would practice scrambling under the tracks to hide for our safety, because there was no place to run away while on the bridge. It was a dangerous tactic, but we were having fun doing it. Of course, one mistake and it would have cost us our lives.

After crossing the bridge, we climbed the hill from the western side. When we went over the hill to the eastern side and about half way down, we came across several foxholes, presumably made by the Marines during their training. Close to one of the foxholes, on a stake about four feet high, was a human skull. We immediately thought that this could be a sacred Hawaiian burial ground. So, we zoomed off the hill in no seconds flat.

The train trestle across Maliko Gulch.   Maui Historical Society photo

We returned to Paia by walking over the Maliko Gulch on the bridge with the rail tracks.

All the hikes we took were in preparation for our 20-mile hiking merit badge. For this 20-mile hike, we walked from Paia through Makawao (there was no town like Pukalani in those days), about four miles, to Ulupalakua Ranch, about 12 miles, and down the Haleakala slope through the pasture to Kihei, about eight miles, and camped overnight. There were a number of skeletons that looked like cows along the way. We finished the hike by returning via the sugar cane fields to Paia, about 10 miles.

It was fun. Good comradeship, friendship flourished and we learned about each others' habits while on our hiking excursions.

In those days there was no such thing as camping permits. We were free to camp and hike wherever we desired.

Also, we heard, from Mr. Stein, about the survival techniques utilized by the servicemen in the jungles when they became isolated from their main unit. To experience and simulate the survival living of our servicemen as members of Troop 45, we hiked to Maalaea from Paia through the cane fields with rice, shoyu, a small frying pan and a piece of string in our backpack. We hiked with the minimum of necessities. For water, we drank from the ditches and punawai. While walking among the tall cane fields, we would imagine that we were lost in the jungle, just like the servicemen in combat. Actually, we felt that we really were lost several times. We walked in the general direction toward Maalaea and used the West Maui Mountains and Haleakala Mountain as our compass. When we came across a punawai or ditch, we would dig for earthworms and attach the worms to the string (no hooks) and fish for guppies. It was easy to hook the guppies. The guppies would swallow one end of the worm, and it was easy to land them. We kept the skinny guppies and threw the fat ones (pregnant and bitter tasting) back into the water. When we had enough lean guppies, we would build a fire and fry the guppies, with shoyu, and eat them with the rice. Boy, when you are hungry, the guppies sure tasted like ono (delicious) real fish.

At one camping outing at Camp Maluhia, we went down the mountain towards the Makamakaole Valley. Instead of turning left through the fence onto the stream to the mauka side, we turned right by the bridge and followed the stream towards the makai side. I don't believe there was a fence at that time. After we ventured about 50 yards from the road through the thick jungle of guava trees, we stumbled upon a large hole of calm water. There was a gentle waterfall cascading down the slippery rocks. We would slide down the slithery rocks and tumble into the water. We kept on sliding until the rocks were almost stripped bare of moss for our comfort. Boy, what fun and entertainment! After the fun, we followed the stream. We were unable to see the end, but we could hear a thundering noise like a huge waterfall falling into the ocean. So we hesitated. Also, we came across several empty splintered wooden containers that were scattered around and in the bushes on the side of the valley. On the bottom of the valley, there was numerous ammunition, with red coloring on the tips of the bullets. We did not handle any bullets, thinking that they could be live. Perhaps the military trucks could have lost the boxes when making the turn. We reported what we found to the Boy Scout office upon our return. We never did return to check if the broken boxes and ammunition were still there.

I was the camp bugler and the lifeguard at the Boy Scout summer camps in 1943 and 1944 at Camp Maluhia. I used to teach some of the younger Scouts to swim.

There were a couple of incidents that stand out in my recollections at the summer camp. One day I asked one of my friends to take my place at the pool as the lifeguard, so that some of my Scout friends and I could go up to a stream to catch opai (fresh water shrimps). There were lots and lots of opai that we scooped with our hands and our handkerchiefs.

Upon our return from the opai gathering expedition, our Boy Scout Executive, Mr. Harold Stein, who was by the poolside, called me. What followed was humiliating, embarrassing, downgrading and made me feel like I was only one inch tall. Mr. Stein chewed me from head to foot and from foot to head and down again from head to foot several times with a stern voice that could easily be heard by all the Scouts around the pool. He bellowed that, "Your job is a lifeguard so that nobody would drown. You were supposed to ask permission from me if you wanted to have a little time off. You had no right to ask someone to take your place." And on and on and on. And to this day, I can still see his face and hear his voice. He had all the reasons in the world to lecture me in that way. And I believe what Mr. Stein drilled into my head made me a better and more responsible person, a better citizen and a better Scout. Thank you, Mr. Stein.

By the way, nobody on the summer camping staff was paid.

In the second event, on my day off, I climbed the mountain mauka of Camp Maluhia by myself to fulfill my curiosity and my adventure-seeking spirit. There was no trail. The sides of the mountain were so steep that should I slip, I would be a dead goner. I kept on climbing to see what was on the other side. At about the three-four thousand foot level, I came upon a flat plateau. What I saw amazed me. It was something like a lost continent, something out of this world. It was flat like a pancake, wet and with steep cliffs all around. There were miniature trees, miniature plants that resembled the silversword plants on Haleakala Mountain and stumped shrubs. I wrote an article as to what I saw and it was published in *The Maui News* with my name on the byline. What I stumbled on was, I believed, the highest peak of the West Maui Mountains, called Pu`u Kukui. When Mr. Stein read that story, he told me that I wasn't supposed to go up there. Mr. Stein's comments gave me the impression that Pu`u Kukui was a sacred place, kapu (keep out). Now I realize it wasn't Pu`u Kukui, but another peak, Eke, and that it too is a special place that wandering hikers should avoid.

Before the summer camp ended in 1944, I attained the rank of Eagle Scout, along with Charles Crane and Wallace Doty of Troop l3, Robert (Propaganda) Nakamoto of Troop 5 and George Sano of Troop 40. The Eagle Scout is the highest achievement a Boy Scout can acquire.

I also served on the Boy Scout camping staff, along with Mr. Stein and Mr. Ohta, on Molokai during the spring break for one week in 1944 as the camp bugler and the lifeguard. There wasn't a swimming pool on Molokai in those days, so all the swimming was at the beach at the Boy Scout summer camp in the wilderness.

One morning on Molokai, while going to the camp, we came across several wild piglets among the trees. We jumped out of the car and ran after them. We were told to be aware of the mother pig that could be nearby, because of its viciousness to protect its young. After chasing them for several minutes between the trees trying to catch at least one piglet, we became exhausted. We didn't realize that the piglets were so nimble and fast. After resting several minutes, we resumed our pursuit. We were able to capture a squealing piglet out of about six and gave it to a friend of Mr. Ohta.

Proving Our Patriotism

The following drama unfolded when my brother, who was working in the main CCC (Civilian Conservation Corps) office in Honolulu, volunteered for the newly formed 442nd Regimental Combat Team in March of 1943. My brother was among thousands who volunteered, to show their patriotism for their beloved county.

We are very much aware of the heroic undertakings the 442nd Regimental Combat Team performed to prove their loyalty to the USA. The 442nd consisted purely of volunteers from the second generation of Japanese Americans. They saw combat in Italy, France and Germany.

There were about 18,143 individual decorations for valor, and the 442nd Regimental Combat Team won the distinction of "The most decorated unit for its size and length of service in the history of the United States."

It is noteworthy what President Harry S. Truman said after he pinned the final Presidential Unit Citation to the colors of the 442nd Regimental Combat Team. The President said, "I can't tell you how much I appreciate the privilege of being able to show you just how much the United States thinks of what you have done…You fought not only the enemy but you fought prejudice…and you won."

Before my brother was shipped out, my mother, who was an Issei (first-generation Japanese), my auntie Ruth Takaki and I went to see the Home Security Officer, Mr. Crane, to obtain permission for my mother to fly to Honolulu to see her son. I cannot recall where his office was; perhaps it was in the old *Maui News* building, on High Street.

My mother was denied permission to fly to see her son, because of her Japanese background.

On the plane, there were curtains that covered all the windows. I saw people parting the curtain to see outside. When I tried to look out, I was instructed not to move the curtain. I felt that I could not look out because of my Japanese heritage.

My auntie and I went to Schofield Barracks, to a place known at that time as Tent City, to see my brother. We talked for a while. It wasn't long because the men were preparing to be shipped out. Before we parted, my brother said, "Study hard," just like a concerned big brother.

When we returned to Maui, I thought to myself, if my mother never sees her son again, I'll never forgive Mr. Crane.

Well, everything turned out super-well, as if the script were written by angelic hands. My brother returned to our mother after receiving a Purple Heart Medal, and I forgave Mr. Crane.

My brother later became a successful lawyer, opened his own law practice, and served as a judge on Kauai under Governor Quinn. It is firmly believed that he became the only judge and lawyer to have emerged from Nashiwa Camp.

Upon graduating from Maui High School in 1945, I was drafted into the Army, and shipped to Ft. McClellan, Alabama, with several of us from Maui, including classmates Robert Matsushita and Ralph Nikaido. And there was Fujio (Fuj) Shibano of Baldwin High School. While at basic training, I felt at home during the forced double-time marches with full field packs, because my legs were in top condition due to all the hikes I took while a Boy Scout. During the forced double-time marches, several soldiers dropped to the side.

After training in the late afternoons, we strolled around the training site and found many training foxholes made by soldiers prior to our arrival. There were dead rattlesnakes in several of the holes. That was the first time we from Hawaii ever saw rattlesnakes. In one instance, as we sat for an orientation class in the woods, an enemy in the form of a live sidewinder (rattlesnake) sidewindered across our class and we naturally frantically jumped up and scrambled to higher ground. We knew then that we were in a training area surrounded by rattlesnakes. Our chairs were long logs made in semicircle, and each row of logs was elevated behind each other.

At 5 feet 4 inches tall, I was the shortest man in the platoon and always held the rear end on all marches. There were men from Virginia, Georgia, Alabama, Louisiana, Mississippi and Texas in our platoon, and they were mostly 6 feet tall. We all talked a little differently, but we understood each other. Anchoring the rear end required me to carry a sign, made of wood, of our outfit wherever we went to train. However, I was able to stay in step with the sky scrapers. Hate to boast, but because of the way he treated and talked to me, I felt that I earned the respect and admiration of our platoon sergeant.

Here I am leaning on a Jeep as a member of the U.S. Army.

The most exciting and hazardous part of our training occurred in a wide-open range where we were instructed to dig individual foxholes. We were warned to dig the foxholes just big enough for our body so we could crouch in a sitting position. After digging the foxholes, a tank would roll over us. When we heard the tank rumbling our way, we would nervously crouch as small as we could with our hands over the muzzle of our rifles to prevent any dirt from entering the chambers and close our eyes tight to keep the dust created by the tank out of our eyes. We had only our steel helmets for protection. If we dug our fox-holes in a sloppy manner and should they ever collapse, or if the tank should drop into the foxholes without our invitation, the steel helmet would have been of no help.

Tossing live hand grenades at an imaginary enemy was fun. The rifle range was a noisy place. Many of us complained about ringing in our ears and that we were half deaf. In fact, my ears are still ringing. After our first day of shooting at the targets with the M1 rifles, our shoulders were numb with pain. Many of us were not accustomed to firing combat rifles like the M1. It was like a mule kicking us on our shoulders whenever we pulled the trigger. In the following days, we took towels to use between our shoulders and the rifle butts. The M1 rifle weighed approximately 9 pounds. With fixed bayonets on our rifles, we would practice on man-sized straw dummies by thrusting the bayonets into the necks of the dummies. We would advance from one dummy to another dummy. We also practiced hand-to-hand combat drills.

Our scheduled 17 weeks of vigorous basic training came to an ab-rupt halt in September of 1945, when the Japanese government signed the unconditional surrender terms under the watchful eyes of General Douglas MacArthur and Allied dignitaries on board the battleship Missouri in Tokyo Bay, Japan, to end the hostilities of World War II. (The ship, "The Mighty Mo," is now a floating museum at Pearl Har-bor.) After completing a more relaxed training, we got orders to go to Fort Snelling.

Whenever I tell the following stories to our swimmers at the pool, they would make funny faces and say ugh, wow, e-e-gh, or utter sounds of disbelief. There was nothing private in the service. Everything was done in the open.

For instance, about 20 of us soldiers would shower together in a single room in the nude and talk to each other while cleansing ourselves. After breakfast, the toilets were usually busy. There were about 15 toilets parallel to each other, with about 8 feet of space in between. While we were doing our chores in emptying our bowels, we would face each other and talk, usually about families, sisters, girl friends, weekend passes, etc. There were no stalls in between the toi-lets and showers. Perhaps in the modern services, they may have in-

49

stalled stalls. Also, in the evenings, especially after lights out, guys would clean their rifles in between the toilets and talk stories with buddies sitting on the thrones.

In Hawaii we never talked or really knew about discrimination. On weekend passes to the big cities, we were exposed and disgustingly came to know what real discrimination was all about. We never did call a Black person a nigger. In fact, we truly didn't know that the word "nigger" ever existed. But in Alabama, at that time, the haoles called the Blacks niggers, and treated them as third-class citizens. On weekend passes, we usually went to Birmingham. On the bus, as a habit, we always moved toward the rear to sit. The bus driver would come to us and tell us to move to the front, because the rear was reserved for niggers only. But we insisted that we didn't mind sitting with the Blacks.

The Blacks were not allowed to enter a restaurant to sit and eat with the haoles. And to see a movie in a theater, the Blacks had to enter through a rear side door and watch the movie from the rear balcony, which was referred to by the haoles as Nigger Heaven. Also, we noticed that whenever a haole was walking on the sidewalk and a Black person was coming from the opposite direction, he would step aside and walk on the street.

It should be emphasized that not all haoles downgraded the Black people and called them niggers. Certainly there were many good and decent haoles in Alabama while we were stationed there. As the true quotation goes, or something like it, "A single rotten apple spoils a barrel of good apples."

We were discriminated against in a way, but not to the extent of how the Blacks were treated. Twice when we went to hotels on separate occasions for rooms, we were told, "No vacancy." As we were relaxing in the lobby, a bunch of haole sailors came in and asked for rooms. They were given rooms. So, we went over to the reservation desk and asked how come they were given rooms. When we asked for rooms again, the clerk, without any explanation, repeated, "No vacancy." We got the picture. We slept on the chairs in the lobby. In the second case, we slept in the basement of a hotel.

After that, we searched for hotels that looked as if they needed our business.

On several occasions, on weekends, I would stay in the camp because I didn't have enough of the green stuff to go sight-seeing. Sometimes my rich buddies would ask me to do their laundry for cash. The dough was welcomed.

After Ft. McClellan, I went to Ft. Snelling, Minnesota, to learn how to write, read and speak Japanese. All the instructors at the language school were haoles, but they could write, read and speak Japanese better than most of us Japanese-Americans from Hawaii. I was impressed.

At Ft. Snelling during the winter months, we were introduced for the first time in our lives to the fluffy white stuff, snow. And it was bitter cold. During our marches from the barracks to the classrooms, it was so shivery that our eyebrows, eyelashes and the hair in our noses would collect ice.

But what we were experiencing in the bone-chilling weather as peace-time soldier marchers at Ft. Snelling cannot be compared as to what the GIs in combat were exposed to in Europe, like the "Battle of the Bulge," fighting in the Italian mountains and in France and in Germany and in the Korean War. These guys really know what freezing cold meant, and we should all be humble and thankful for their dreaded, gut-wrenching victories in their hand-to-hand battles. Our nation is what we are today, "THE LAND OF THE FREE AND THE HOME OF THE BRAVE," because of their heroic achievements.

The contrasting weather that we encountered at Alabama and Minnesota was like day and night, from extreme hot to extreme cold.

On a weekend, we ventured onto the frozen Mississippi River and like the movies and cartoons where we see people cutting holes in the frozen ice to fish, we copied. The ice was too thick to cut with nothing but a stick. So, we used a hole that was abandoned by people before we came. We had nothing but a shining safety pin that someone had. We tied the safety pin to a string and playfully dangled the shining safety pin in the hole. And to our amazement, we caught an eight-inch carp. We threw the carp back into the hole. There were several frozen dead carps, about 18 inches long, on the ice that people had discarded.

I knew that I was destined to go to Japan after the schooling at Ft. Snelling. My father, who had two brothers living in Japan, wanted me to meet them.

51

However, I was determined to go to Germany, because when my brother was in Europe, he wrote about visiting Rome and seeing the Colosseum, climbing the leaning Tower of Pisa, visiting Paris and taking part in the liberation of the Dachau concentration camp. I wanted to visit the places that my brother saw and visited. So I took my discharge and re-enlisted for three years to go to Europe. When I re-enlisted, the Army gave me $500 as mustering-out pay and a 30-day furlough at home.

When I came home in March 1946 for my 30-day furlough, I gave my mother the $500. And, was she happy! Perhaps that was the only time she ever saw and handled $500. We went immediately to the Paia Store, which was located opposite the mill, and bought an electric stove to replace the ancient kerosene stove. My father and sisters were ecstatic.

While I was on furlough, the Scouts of Troop 45 were looking for a Scoutmaster. Sakae Uehara (now a retired doctor) and I went to see Willard (Lanky) Matsumoto, a veteran of the 442nd Regimental Combat Team and a former Scout in Troop 30, to become the Scoutmaster. Lanky must have just come home from work, because he was sitting on the porch, taking his shoes off. Lanky was a sugarcane field luna (supervisor). Kinda big shot, being a Japanese American.

Lanky knew who we were. We asked him straight, "Would you please become the Scoutmaster of Troop 45?" With his gentle smile, and with a bit of hesitation, he said, "OK." He asked us where we met and how many boys were involved. Under his leadership, Troop 45 became a first-class outfit and increased in membership.

Lanky became so deeply involved in the Scouting movement that he became the Scout Executive on the Big Island. After the retirement of Mr. Jim Ohta, Lanky became the Boy Scout Executive of Maui County and after many years, retired in that position. Thank you, Lanky!

After my 30-day furlough was over, I was scheduled to leave Maui on April 1, 1946, for Schofield Barracks and subsequently to Camp Kilmer, New Jersey and on to Germany.

Something strange happened on April 1. It was like an April fool's joke. Only, it was no April fool's joke. There was no bus service to take me to the Kahului Naval Air Station, where I was scheduled to fly out of Maui. So my parents inquired about a taxi service. I walked to the usual bus stop at the Nashiwa Bakery, where the taxi picked me up.

The taxi driver informed me that a tidal wave struck Maui, and the bus service was suspended. He drove down Baldwin Avenue toward Lower Paia. While going to Lower Paia, I saw my father, with other plantation workers, in front of the Paia Meat Market, just mauka of the Paia Store. I learned later that they were meeting in anticipation of a strike against the sugar company. I waved but he did not wave back, perhaps wondering who the stranger was waving from inside the taxi.

The driver did not go all the way down Baldwin Avenue. Instead, he turned left onto the cane field dirt road, explaining that the main highway was closed due to the tidal wave. After zigzagging through the cane fields, we emerged on the Hana Highway, close to the playground and Baldwin Park. What we saw drew attention to the fact that the tidal wave that struck Maui was overwhelming, with destructive force beyond imagination.

My friend Mac's house is behind the truck.   Maui Historical Society photo.

Smack in the middle of Hana Highway was the home of my class-mate, Mac Magarifuji, a former outstanding football and basketball player from Maui High School. The home was originally on the left side of the highway going toward Hana and it was the first home along

53

the row of homes. Then I knew why there were no buses running that morning. It must have been a truly titanic wave that surged over the sand bank to lift the entire home off its foundation and gently deposit the home in the middle of the highway. The home showed no sign of damage from our vantage point inside the cab. It certainly is a mystery as to why only one home was affected.

Many deaths were attributed to the April 1 tidal wave. Around the territory, 159 were dead or missing. On Maui, 14 died.

After the debris was cleared at the Naval Air Station, we were able to take off. From the air, we could see the devastation caused by the tidal wave. The buildings that were still standing had been swept off their foundations; the majority of the wooden structures were cut to pieces and scattered for yards. Water was all over the naval facilities. I was rather familiar with the Naval Air Station, because that is where we took our physical examinations upon being drafted. The Naval Air Station was where we know today as the Kahului Airport.

Because of the disastrous tidal wave experience in 1946, *The Maui News* applied for a radio station license, citing that the people on Maui had no warning method to inform them of any impending natural danger. *The Maui News* successfully obtained the radio station license and received the call sign of KMVI-Radio (which means "Maui Valley Isle"; 550 on the radio dial) and was the first radio station to go on the air in Maui County.

On my way to Camp Kilmer, I visited my friends at Ft. Snelling. When I had left Ft. Snelling in February to come home for my 30-day furlough, there was lots of snow and the trees were naked, not a single leaf on the branches. In early April, upon my return, the snow was gone and the trees were all dressed up with green leaves covering every inch of the once bare trees. Boy, what a beautiful contrast.

While I was at Camp Kilmer, we visited New York City to take in the sights, such as the Empire State Building, Statue of Liberty, China Town, etc, etc. We also visited a women's college within walking distance. When we went there, several young ladies were shooting bow and arrows. All the arrows were stuck around the target but we did not see a bull's-eye. We asked whether we could try to use the bow and arrows. They were very friendly and told us to go ahead. We tried, but

54

the arrows would fly in all directions, not even close to the target. The ladies had a good laugh watching us.

Swimming for My Country

In 1946 in Germany, as a member of the US Army Signal Corps, my first job was as a stenographer for the local Military Court in Heidelberg, since I knew shorthand learned at Maui High. While serving as a court reporter, the Athletic Officer of our battalion, who checked my background when I was drafted, called and said that he wanted me to swim for the swimming team.

I was placed on temporary duty with the swimming team and participated in the EUCOM (European Command) swimming championships in Nuremberg. After the championships, I was selected as a member of the EUCOM all-star team. Following a week of recreational training in Munich, we traveled in cars to Prague, Czechoslovakia, for an Inter-Allied swimming meet. We didn't swim well, as most of the swimmers in the military were not in good swimming shape.

Driving to Prague, there were many fruit trees along the roads, like pears and apples, where one could stop and enjoy them. The roads leading into Vienna, Austria and the country roads in Germany were also lined with the fruits.

On our way to Czechoslovakia, we visited the notorious former Dachau concentration camp, where thousands of Jews were tortured and put to death. We entered the concentration camp via the main entrance with a huge archway. On the immediate right after we entered were two incinerators where the bodies of the dead were cremated. On the rear right of the incinerators was a wall full of bullet holes. We were told that the victims were lined up at the wall and shot, and the bodies would fall into a ditch in front of them and were covered with dirt. Next to the incinerators was a building where the victims were ushered in and were told that they were going to take a shower. Instead of water coming from above, deadly gas would pour into the room. There was a room where the victims were ordered to strip nude before they were escorted into the room for a shower.

Just outside of the incinerator area were two parallel barbed wire fences. In between the two barbed-wire fences was a ditch full of water, which made it difficult for anyone trying to escape. Inside the second barbed-wire fence were a countless number of structures like dog houses. The poor Jews were crammed into them with no leg room.

In the main compound, there were several army-type barracks that housed the thousands of victims. To the far right of the army-type barracks, close to another barbed-wire fence, were wooden posts about 6 feet tall. The victims were tied to the posts to be tortured or hung with their hands elevated and their feet lashed to the posts until they died.

In 1984, I took my whole family to Germany so that our children could meet their mother's side of the family and to celebrate my wife's sister's golden anniversary. We also traveled to Austria, Hungary, Switzerland, Italy and France.

On our way to Vienna, we stopped at the Dachau Concentration Memorial Camp, located just outside of Munich. What I saw at the Dachau Concentration Memorial Camp in 1984 and in 1946 were two drastically different versions. When we tried to enter the main gate in 1984, the way we did as members of the EUCOM swimming team in 1946, we were met by security guards and were told that we could not enter. We were instructed to enter the memorial via a different entrance.

When we entered the memorial, all the army-type barracks were gone, except the concrete foundations. All the dog-house type of structures were gone. The incinerators and the buildings next to them were still there.

The 442nd Regimental Combat Team liberated the Dachau Concentration Camp, and my brother recalls that the prisoners were Jewish holocaust victims. "The German guards had fled and abandoned the camp. One of our men from Honolulu shot the gate open to release the prisoners. They were wearing black-and-white striped prison suits and round caps on their heads. They shuffled weakly out of the prison compound. They were like skeletons—all skin and bones. Our men entered the prison compound and saw several dead bodies piled up like logs ready to be burned in the ovens, some of which were still warm."

In Czechoslovakia, we traveled as a group. The top ranking officer was a major, followed by a captain and one or two lieutenants. I believe I was the only private. Whenever or wherever we went or ate, we sat together. The other Allied servicemen ate separately from their officers, and they were surprised and rather shocked as we Americans sat together and talked to each other as if we were all equal in rank.

In Prague, I remember visiting an ancient castle. Upstairs in a sealed room, there were soldiers guarding every doorway. In the room everything was made of solid gold: the statues, chandeliers, tables, chairs, window frames, etc.

We also walked across a beautiful bridge highlighted with life-like statues of the 12 disciples that arched over the famous Blue Danube River.

At the restaurant in the hotel, we didn't know what the menus contained in terms of what to order. The major, fluent in German, asked the waiters several times what type of food the menu contained. The waiters, all men, would shrug their shoulders and gesture with their hands indicating that they did not understand German. So, we ordered different plates to see what they were and kept track of the varied types of dishes.

About three days later, when we became familiar and friendly with the waiters and with the major consistently talking in German, the waiters started to respond in German. Things became easier for us. When the major asked why they did not speak German when we first came in the restaurant, they said that since the Germans occupied Czechoslovakia for a number of unpleasant years, they wanted to forget the German language.

When we entered the competitive swimming pool in Prague, there was a breath analyzer. There was a graph-like chart where one could see how far a swimmer could blow the red marker in the tube. The tube was gradually elevated on the right and ended on the top with a red bulb. I assumed that the ultimate power in the lungs was for the red marker to hit the red bulb. We were all required to blow into the tube. We did not see anybody reach the red bulb. We tried but most of us Americans were barely able to pass the half-way point. Most of the Europeans surpassed us. It clearly showed that the Europeans had stronger lung power than we Americans.

When three of us were strolling in a courtyard one day, a man came out of a building and gestured with his hands and head to come. We went over to him, and he said that he was an editor of a newspaper and wanted to interview us. He directed his questions mostly to me. He asked if I were an American. I told him, "Yes, I am an American." It seems as though I was the first Japanese-American he ever saw. Of course, I certainly didn't look like my haole swim mates. He then asked me how I was treated. He spoke fairly good English. I replied, "OK." And he said in a questionably way, "OK?" I answered with a positive, "OK!" I felt like he was tempting me to say something negative about the USA. He was talking to the wrong person!

He then motioned the three of us to follow him into the building. At the entrance of the building was a hammer and sickle. One of us said, "This is a Communist newspaper. We don't want to talk to an editor of a Communist newspaper." He denied that he was a Communist. Out of pure curiosity, we entered the building. On the wall of a large room that looked like a conference room, was a picture of Mr. Joseph Stalin, ruler of Russia. Under his picture was the insignia of the hammer and sickle. We almost shouted in unison, "This is a Communist newspaper!" We started to walk away. The editor followed. As we continued to walk to the exit, he kept on repudiating that he wasn't a Communist. After we left the building, the editor standing by the doorway, sustained his assertion that he wasn't a Communist. Perhaps he was telling the truth. Maybe he was not a Communist.

I do remember a somewhat embarrassing romantic fling by a bold young wahine in Prague. The cute young lady, about 15 years of age and perhaps with her young brother of about 12, kept following me from the parking lot to the pool. She would also follow me and the rest of us swimmers from the pool to the car. She kept saying, "Ich liebe dich, Ich liebe dich." I didn't know what that meant at that time. That went on for about two days. The major, who understood and spoke German, didn't say a word. It is very possible that the major knew exactly what was going on and could have kept things to himself. The major could have been chuckling to himself under his breath and was having a silent amusing time, listening to the wahine for two days. When I asked him what she was saying, he would smile and with a rascal wink of his eye, said, "You are lucky. She is telling you 'I love you, I love you'." Lucky? Love me? Why me, an innocent skinny sol-

58

dier who never kissed a wahine in 19 years of my young life? My swim mates were much taller and better looking than me. It sure didn't make any sense as to why the under-aged wahine fell for me. I asked the Major to tell her that I wasn't interested and to stop following me. I don't know what he told her in German, but she continued to haunt me until we left Prague. She must be must be about 78 years of age now. At this late calendar, I wonder if she still remembers and thinks of me?

I won first place in this swimming competition in Heidelberg, where I broke records in the 200- and 400-meter freestyle.

For awards in the EUCOM championships, instead of receiving medals for the top three swimmers, we received merchandise. I received a Rolex watch, my first wristwatch in my life, for first place, and lesser known watches for the other places which I gave to team-mates who did not win any.

In 1947, I was sent by our commanding officer to participate in a two-week swimming clinic in Munich. The head instructor was Coach Bob Kiputh, a multiple USA Olympic swimming head coach. Coach Kiputh was the head swimming coach at Yale University. Along with Mr. Kiputh, there were Mr. Peterson, swimming head coach at the Northwestern University and former Olympic and world-class record sprinter, Otto Jarertz.

It was a wonderful experience swimming under Coach Kiputh and watching Otto demonstrate his powerful kick. I was asked to swim the freestyle and backstroke, and while I was swimming, Coach Kiputh was saying something to the class about my swimming. I don't know what he was talking about, but I hope it was something nice. All the swimmers would race Otto, but with only his sensational kicking, he would beat us with ease. Swimming against Otto was like being a cat in a duel with a tiger. Otto was a dominating figure at six feet eight inches.

While talking to the gathering one day, Coach Kiputh gave a ster-ling testimony about Keo Nakama, Coach Sakamoto's first national champion and holder of a number of world swimming records. Mr. Ki-puth said, and I remember his words as if his comments were made only yesterday, "When you see Keo swim, you don't want him to stop swimming. You want to see him swim and swim and swim and swim. He was so graceful and fluent, that it is like reading a good book and you hate to stop. You read the book page after page after page after page until you finish."

That is about the best tribute a person can receive from a respected World Swimming Hall of Famer, Coach Bob Kiputh, or anybody else.

Coach Kiputh was curious and wanted to see the training site and how the German Olympic Gold Medal sprinter trained in Munich. Coach Kiputh was anxious to learn how the German was able to be-come an Olympic sprint champion training in a 20-meter pool. For the first time the two American swimming coaches, Mr. Kiputh and Mr. Peterson, witnessed the resistance type of training via a fishing pole. Ah, yes, it was an authentic fishing pole, anchored to the deck. The swimmer would wrap a harness around his waist, attach a fishing line to the flexible pole, and swim.

Today, there are many modern versions of the ancient fishing pole technique.

After the 1948 EUCOM championships, I was one of the fortunate eight swimmers to accompany Lt. (Doctor) Sammy Lee, Gold Medal winner of the 1948 Olympic platform competition, for a two-week demonstration tour of swimming and lifesaving techniques throughout the Army bases in Germany. Mr. Babe Papish, head of the American Red Cross in Germany, accompanied the group as the PR (Public Relations) and PIO (Public Information Office) representative. I believe Mr. Papish was an instructor at the University of Texas as a civilian. We traveled in first-class fashion for two weeks. We slept in first-class hotels, ate and traveled like kings. We visited the military posts in Furstenfeldbruck, Munich, Giessen, Wiesbaden, Frankfurt, and many other cities scattered in Germany.

It is a great wonder what privileges and favors a celebrity like Sammy Lee can generate.

I believe Sammy Lee is credited as the first diver in the world to negotiate a three-and-a half dive from the 10-meter platform.

After two weeks of leisure swimming and demonstrations, we journeyed to Vienna, Austria, where we were invited to swim in the Austrian swimming championships. The main attraction was Sammy Lee, the 1948 Olympic high-board diving Gold Medal champion. Sammy Lee's exhibitions stole the swimming competitions and overshadowed the swimming accomplishments of the Austrian swimming champions. We participated in the championships, but after two weeks of living like kings, we were happy and fortunate just to finish the races.

After the meet, we were treated to a rare opera presentation. Most of us were not enthused to attend the opera. But we all went. That was the first opera we all witnessed and, personally, I genuinely enjoyed the costumes, the singing and the acting.

When we were walking on the main street in Vienna, we saw a sign about Sammy Lee's diving. We entered to see how the pictures looked. To our surprise, there wasn't a single picture of Sammy Lee's exhibition. The only pictures we saw were the Austrian swimming champions. The sign on the front of the photographic store was a come-along bait for customers.

Also, we entered a vegetable and fruit court. Seeing a stand displaying delicious looking fruits of peaches, plums, pears, apples, etc., we were tempted to purchase. Like all Americans, we liked to feel the firmness or softness of the peaches and plums. When we were feeling the peaches, the merchant slapped our hands and said, "Nein, nein." In English, "No, no." We were informed that the custom in Austria, and perhaps in other European countries, is that no one is allowed to feel the fruits. You buy them as they are.

After the swimming episode in 1948, I was transferred to the Frankfurt Military Post. Upon learning that the Army newspaper, *The Occupation Chronicle,* the eyes and ears of the Frankfurt Military Post, was looking for a sports reporter, I applied and got the assignment. After about a month as a sports reporter, I became the sports editor. As the sports editor, I was assigned a German driver to take me wherever there was a sporting activity, and it covered a wide area of Germany.

When I was stationed in Frankfurt, the Japanese Olympic Team came to Germany to relax and have its swimmers put on an exhibition. The Athletic Officer, Lt. Allen, called one Sunday morning and asked me if I could speak Japanese, because there was no one in the Special Services that could speak and understand the Japanese language. The Athletic Officer was concerned because the welfare of the Japanese Olympic Team came under his jurisdiction.

I told him that I was out of touch with the Japanese language and was not fluent, but I thought that I could manage the language with the Japanese.

When we went to the hotel, the Japanese Olympic Team was on a tour of the Rhine River and was scheduled to return momentarily. When the team entered the hotel lobby, in desperation, I hollered at the top of my lungs: "Can anybody speak English?" A gentleman from the back of the crowd raised his hand and replied: "Yes, I can speak English. I am a Harvard graduate." He spoke loud and clear like a professor. That solved the Athletic Officer's anxiety and especially mine.

While the exhibition was going on, the Athletic Officer asked if I wanted to swim alongside "the flying fish of Fujiyama," Hironoshin Furuhashi, not against him but with him. After talking with the Japanese coach, he consented to my swimming with Furuhashi. It was an honor just to swim next to a world champion.

In 1950, during the Korean conflict, there was a Berlin blockade. Nothing was able to enter Berlin by road or train because the Russians installed a strict blockade on all means of ground transportation. All the Allied forces (British, French and Americans) were affected. All the food and the necessary items of survival were flown in via air.

The American, British and French rift with the Russians was at the height of the undeclared war tabbed as the Cold War.

We flew into Berlin to compete in a swim meet. On the way out, we were able to leave by train. At the Russian checkpoint, Russian soldiers with rifles entered our compartment and requested to see our dog tags. The American officers were rather reluctant at first. They said that it was humiliating that we were treated as if we were prisoners, but instructed the rest of us to display our dog tags. The Russians solders didn't show any signs of hostility. They half-smiled and said, perhaps jokingly, in German, "We are comrades. The trouble makers are the officers (politicians)."

(I still have in my possession one of the two original dog tags that I showed to the Russians.)

Perhaps the Russian soldiers wanted to be positive that we were real Americans soldiers by showing our dog tags and not civilians in American uniforms who were trying to escape from the rigid Russian-occupied zone.

Since the blockade of Berlin by the Russians was not working to their advantage, due to the combined successful air lift of the Allied Forces, it was lifted.

In 1951, after the EUCOM swimming championships in Berlin, as members of the US Armed Forces Team, we flew to London, England, in a huge flying box car, courtesy of the US Air Force, to participate in the Britannia Shield competitions. We were billeted in a British Royal Air Force base, and that is where we were initially introduced to television via a black-and-white eight-inch screen. The TV was located in a corner and was surrounded by more than a dozen British airmen in the recreational room. At that time, television was treated more like a curiosity and a novelty item, rather than entertainment.

Before swimming the 1500-meter freestyle, I ate a whole chocolate candy bar, thinking that it might give me an extra boost. Instead of the extra boost, I inherited an agonizing chest pain about half way through the race. I wanted to stop, but was kind of ashamed to give up in the middle of the race, so I continued to finish the longest swim of my young career. I came in number one last. When I painfully crawled out of the pool, the officer in charge of the Britannia Shield group shook his head in disapproval, never realizing how much I suffered while swimming. That incident displayed by the officer has always been a reminder, as a coach, never to play down a swimmer if he or she doesn't perform up to expectation. There may have been circumstances unknown to the coach that could have affected the swimmer.

A Lifeguard's Reward

About a year after I took the sports editor job, I received a call from the athletic officer of the Giessen Military Post to become a lifeguard at one of the pools. I accepted and transferred to the Special Services. A year later, the athletic officer, Capt. Paul Davis, was transferred to the Frankfurt Military Post, a much larger military post than the Giessen Military Post. I went along with him and, before leaving Giessen, I received the stripes of a staff sergeant.

At Frankfurt, I became the supervisor of an indoor pool in Fechenheim. There was an assistant solder lifeguard and a civilian helper. There were 13 German employees under my care. The indoor pool consisted of a 20-meter pool and men's dressing room on the main floor with showers. There also was a recreational and exercise room. The second floor housed the women's dressing room, steam bath room with two massage tables, showers, a balcony and my living quarters. There were about 15 private bath tubs on the third floor and the living quarters for the caretaker of the pool and building. The cellar had six private showers and the boiler room.

After the pool closed at 9 p.m., I usually gave permission for the workers to swim or to utilize the shower facilities. One evening, as I was walking on the pool deck, one of the female workers was swimming the breaststroke. Another worker playfully jumped in front of her, and when she opened her mouth for air, instead of air, she gulped a bucket full of water and sank to the bottom of the pool like a rock. I stopped and watched a few seconds. When she did not move, I jumped into the water to bring her up to the surface for air.

Before I left Germany in 1952, the lady who sank to the bottom of the pool, Wilma Eschmann, became Mrs. Spencer Shiraishi, for 50 years.

However, before we could get married, there were several obstacles we had to hurdle. My wife was a Catholic, and I was a Protestant. Problems in interfaith and interracial marriage never did enter our minds when we decided to become one. My wife said that even though she was a Catholic, she was not a really strong Catholic.

We went to see a Catholic chaplain to seek his advice and opinion. The Catholic chaplain said that if we got married in his chapel, all of our children must be raised as Catholics. I thought at that time that my children should have a choice to select their own faiths. We thanked the chaplain and informed him that we would talk things over.

After we left the church, my would-be wife, on her own, said that our children should decide for themselves as to what church they want to attend. So, our two minds were welded into one.

We then went to the Protestant chaplain for his opinion. The Protestant chaplain confirmed that if we got married in the Catholic chapel, our children must be raised as Catholics. He suggested that, to avoid any turmoil in her family, we should get married in a civil ceremony. We both felt that it was an ideal solution. My wife came from a family of 11, and she was the second youngest.

But before we could tie the knot, I wrote to my parents that I was going to marry a haole (German). Way back in the ancient time of the plantation days, interracial marriage was never heard of or tolerated, or was whispered about in a hushed tone. When I think of the days at Nashiwa Camp, I do not recall any in interracial unions.

I received a disturbing letter from one of my sisters, who wrote on behalf of my mother. My mother, because of her old-fashioned idea that an ideal marriage should be between two of the same racial origin, really put a damper on my desire to marry the wahine of my choice. My sister even hinted that there were wahines looking forward to my return to Maui.

Well, according to the letter, my mother said without any reservations, if I marry a German, not to come home. That really, really felled me. It was like a dagger striking at my heart.

I never did tell that to my would-be wife. And I never did tell her even after we were happily married.

I answered, after calmly gathering my thoughts, in no uncertain terms, that if she didn't want me to return home with my German wife, she would never see me or her grandchildren, ever.

After a few days I received a letter from my sister saying that my mother apologized and would welcome her German would-be daughter-in-law and me with open arms.

That opened the heavenly gate to our joyous civil marriage ceremony in the office of the Burgermeister (mayor) of Frankfurt on April 23, 1952.

My wife inherited a reddish-blond hair, called strawberry blond. Very pretty. There is a story behind why I wanted to marry a wahine with reddish-blond hair. Sometime back, I saw a movie with Greer Garson and Walter Pidgeon titled, I believe, *Random Harvest.* Greer Garson was a striking beauty with her strawberry blond hair, and I fell in love with that colored hair.

So, when I became the supervisor at the indoor pool, lo and behold, to my amazement, there was my future bride selling Coke behind a Coke stand, with her strawberry blond hair.

Wow, what a coincidence. It was like a God-sent offering. It was love at first sight for me. My wife confided in me later that is how she felt when she first saw me. When two attractions merge into one, something was bound to occur. And it did: Marriage!

Wilma Eschmann became my bride in 1952.

Our spirited and successful interfaith and interracial celebration rose above all doubts of failure, discrimination and intolerance. It was like a story-book setting made in Hollywood and in Heaven.

We attended the Kahului Union Church together and produced four youngsters into our world. Our son, Spencer Jr., modeled his marriage after mine in an interracial ceremony by marrying a beauty of Hawaiian-Chinese ancestry from California, Ululani Smith. Her parents originally came from Hana, Maui. Their children are Hawaiian, Chinese, Japanese and German. My other grandchildren, Lani's daughter, Maile, and Erika's son, Cameron, are one-fourth Japanese and three-fourths Caucasian. They live with their families in Colorado.

At this time, I would like to express my deepest gratitude and admiration to my German wife of 50 years. My wife, Wilma, stood by me without any complaints while we shared the same home with my parents for about six months. She utilized the same toilet house we became accustomed to while we were youngsters. My wife adjusted to our local customs without a whimper, like eating kim chee, sashimi, poke, sushi, octopus, bagon, kalua pig, lau lau, lomi salmon, poi, etc., and was soon loved by my parents.

At potluck gatherings at the church or at the Maui Swim Club's annual Christmas togetherness at the beach every year, my wife made her usual delicious and sought-after German potato pancakes. The potato pancakes are sorely missed by those who were fortunate enough to have eaten them.

My wife never discouraged me from volunteering my time as a swimming coaching for about 50 years while she was on this world. My wife was a faithful, tolerant and a happy companion to be with. Sure miss her!

Back to the USA

Before leaving Germany in early October of 1952, I went to see my CO (commanding officer) to tell him that I might make the Army my career and ask for his advice. He gave me a piece of paper to fill in. In part, the paper gave me three choices as to where I would prefer to be stationed. The first question was: "Where do you want to be stationed?" My answer was: "Schofield Barracks." Question number two: "What is your second choice?" I answered: "West Coast." I left the third choice blank.

My wife and I, with other war brides and their soldier husbands, left Frankfurt in early October of 1952. We traveled by train through Switzerland to Leghorn, Italy. We boarded a troop transport, and our first stop was at Casablanca, Morocco. We stayed overnight, and that gave us an opportunity to go sight-seeing and shopping around Casablanca. We visited the exact location where President Franklin Delano Roosevelt, Mr. Winston Churchill, Prime Minister of Great Britain, and Mr. Joseph Stalin of Russia met in their historic three-power summit conference.

After our pleasant stop at Casablanca, we hightailed across the Atlantic Ocean to the Mainland. As I remember, the ship was huge, with three smoke stacks. The top of the ship was crowded with loud barking German shepherd dogs, perhaps for the big brasses who were going home. All the wives of the servicemen were below deck and we GIs were stuck at the bottom of the ship. I believe we all became seasick, staying at the bottom of the ship.

After about five days on the ocean, we docked at the Brooklyn Naval Shipyard. We stayed in the barracks for about a week, waiting for our car to arrive from Bremerhaven, Germany. While we waited, my wife and I visited our National Capitol, Arlington National Cemetery, Lincoln Memorial, Washington Memorial, the White House, the Empire State Building, the Statue of Liberty, Times Square, etc. It was a thrilling adventure for my wife to see all the cherished memorials and the tourist attractions of her adopted country.

When our car arrived, we drove to Chicago through scenic states. We traveled leisurely through New York, New Jersey, Delaware, Pennsylvania, Virginia, Maryland, Ohio and Indiana. We went through the Lincoln Tunnel and took in the sights. It was a beautiful drive in October, with the leaves changing colors. We also visited Valley Forge, the Civil War battlefield at Gettysburg and the Lincoln Statue and the spot where President Abraham Lincoln delivered his immortal speech.

We stopped in Pittsburgh, Pennsylvania, to visit my former classmate Richard Ikeda and his wife Shirley. They were kind enough to offer dinner, on their probably tight budget. Richard was enrolled at a dental school at the University of Pittsburgh, and I knew his address because we used to correspond with each other while I was stationed in Germany. After graduating from the dental school, Richard opened his dental practice at the Ikeda Store building, owned by his parents, in Lower Paia.

After two days and nights on the road, we arrived at my brother's apartment in Chicago and met his wife, Fumi, his infant son, Marshall, and my sister Jean, who was attending Northwestern University. My brother was finishing his studies to become a lawyer.

While at the Brooklyn Naval Shipyard, I had received my assignment to my next tour of duty. Instead of going to Schofield Barracks as my first choice or to the West Coast, I had orders to report to Camp Crowder, Missouri. So I left my wife in Chicago with my brother, his wife and son and my sister and reported to Camp Crowder.

When my discharge papers came, I was asked if I wanted to re-enlist. My answer was an immediate, "No, thank you." I received my honorable discharge from the military in early December, 1952, at Camp Crowder.

I returned to Chicago after my discharge and, with my GI Bill of Rights, enrolled in an electronics school. While attending school, I was employed as a lifeguard from 3 p.m. to 9 p.m., six days a week, by the City and County of Chicago at Montrose Beach during the summer. I believe I was credited with potentially preventing three drownings. I was paid the hefty sum of $250 a month. At that time, the Montrose Beach and the yacht harbor recreational facility were in first-class condition. I also worked part-time in an electronic shop during the winter months.

On my first day of work as a lifeguard, a tidal wave struck the shoreline of Lake Michigan and made huge headlines. This phenomenon is believed to be the first time a tidal wave ever occurred on Lake Michigan. Many fishermen were swept into the lake. The beach was closed, and we dragged the Montrose Beach yacht harbor with hooks for bodies. We did not retrieve any bodies, but a couple of bodies floated to the surface several days later.

The supervisor at the Montrose Beach was Mr. Stockdale. He was about 5 feet 7, built solid and barrel-chested and probably in his fifties. He must have been the supervisor at that beach for many, many years. Mr. Stockdale was very strict. On the first day after the tidal wave, he summoned all the lifeguards and told us that we are dealing with human lives, and we must be alert and be aware of our surroundings at all times. We were assigned shifts of three hours each. We sat on the lifeguard stands for one hour and then rotated to the life boats for an hour and had the third hour off. I usually did my homework on my time off.

There were about four lifeguard stands situated 10 yards from the waterline, located equidistant from each other, and four lifeboats about 30-50 yards from the shoreline, just opposite of the lifeguard stands. We were ordered to have our hands on the oars at all times so that we

70

could respond right away in an emergency. We had strict orders not to talk to anybody. If a person would ask a question, the person was referred to the captain of the lifeguard crew. The captain was dressed entirely in red for easy recognition and sat or stood by the office close to the telephone. We hardly saw the supervisor. He was in his office most of the time.

On an inclement day, two of us lifeguards were assigned to a special duty at another beach. We went there on a motor boat. When we arrived at the beach, there was a crowd seemingly enjoying playing in the rough surf. There was a sign posted: "NO SWIMMING, DANGEROUS UNDERCURRENT. NO LIFEGUARDS." But the people just disregarded the precautionary sign. We placed ourselves opposite of each other, with no lifeguard uniforms. I sat on a pile of rocks. While surveying the crowd, I noticed two youngsters on separate occasions, about 10 years old, struggling to get to the shore. They were slowly being dragged deeper into the lake by the undercurrent. They would walk slowly towards the beach when the waves would break forward, and when the waves would recede, they would fight the waves, struggling to go towards the shore. I could see their worried faces, and they seemed to be getting panicky. I jumped in and helped them to go forward with the waves. I told them not to fight the waves, but push forward with the waves. They thanked me.

On a more scary assistance, I saw two swimmers about 50 yards offshore. One was trying to help another swimmer. I could see them disappearing and appearing between the huge waves. I jumped in and kept my eyes focused on them. When I reached them, I asked if they needed help. The person who seemed to be in trouble said, "Yes."

So, utilizing my Boy Scout knowledge in the tired swimmer's carry (there may be a different version now), I turned around and faced the shore and instructed the person to keep his elbows straight and to put his hands on my shoulders and his legs on my hips. He did exactly that. I would then swim the breaststroke toward the shore. However, whenever a wave would engulf us, we would lose contact. We did that twice. It didn't help. Then I went in front of him, which was rather dangerous, but he wasn't drowning, just tired. I placed my hand with my elbow stiff on his chest and told him to grab my arm. But whenever a wave would come over, we would tumble over, and he would let go of my arm and lose contact.

We were both getting tired, but not exhausted. This time, with my hand on his chest, and him hanging on to my arm, I would swim the side stroke, and whenever I saw a huge wave coming, I would duck under the water and lift him up as high as I could so that he could keep his face above the water. In that way we didn't lose contact. We were able to reach the shore in that fashion.

After he was safely on shore, I asked him, "Why didn't you yell for help?" He said he was ashamed. With that experience, I always tell the Scouts in my swimming and lifesaving classes that whenever you need help, not to be ashamed to call for help.

The American Red Cross manual and the *Boy Scout Handbook* on swimming and lifesaving did not have any information as to what I underwent. It just became a method of common-sense improvising in a real life drama.

When we returned to Montrose Beach, the other lifeguard reported what he observed. I did not receive a medal or commendation, but was happy to have helped with an appreciation of a healthy thank-you handshake.

It is difficult for people in Hawaii to imagine waves reaching 3 to 5 feet in height at Lake Michigan. And when the waves generated to about 5 feet, the bathers would swarm into the water and just jump up and down with the rise and fall of the tide. There was no room for people to swim or to body surf. And the beach was packed with humanity. We had to be very, very careful not to step on a body whenever we changed shifts.

After the crowd dispersed from the beach at closing time, we would walk slowly and sift through the sand looking for coins. On the average, each one of us would gather about five dollars in coins every day.

While schooling in Chicago, my wife and I became the proud parents of a beautiful daughter, Leilani, in 1954. She was followed by Margaret (Margie) in 1957, Erika in 1959 and Spencer Jr. in 1962, all born on Maui.

Outside my parents' home in Paia, Wilma and Leilani pose with my father, Ikuji, mother, Tomo, and grandmother, Takaki.

Home to Maui, and Back to Scouting

After serving in the Army for over seven years and going to an electronics school in Chicago, I wanted to return to Maui in late December of 1954 and seek employment. Plus, my sister Jonsie (Jean) was scheduled to be wedded to a hulk of a man, handsome Eugene Yamamoto, on Christmas Day, in 1954, at the Iao Congregational Church.

We drove from Chicago via Route 66 to San Francisco to catch the plane to Maui. We drove through Illinois, Missouri, Oklahoma, Texas, New Mexico, Arizona and California. The most interesting spot we visited was the Meteor National Crater Park in Arizona. It is reported that the crater was created by a huge meteor.

It is really difficult to comprehend that we drove from coast to coast without a single misfortune. We were truly blessed. Thank you!

73

Once back on Maui, I had an interview with Mr. Crane, editor and publisher of *The Maui News,* and Mr. Richard Mawson, who was the KMVI-Radio and KMVI-TV station manager, for a job. While interviewing in Mr. Mawson's office, Mr. Crane never had the slightest clue that I once was not going to forgive him for denying my mother a chance to see her son.

I started to work part time for KMVI-TV atop Mt. Haleakala. After a while, I was employed full time and then became the chief engineer for KMVI-Radio, KMVI-TV and *The Maui News.* I became a member of the Kahului Union Church, where in time I served three years on the Board of Trustees, three years on the Christian Education Board, as president of the church and the Men's Fellowship and two years on the Board of Deacons. Also, I co-chaired, along with Don Hughes, the building committee that was responsible for the completion of Puaaiki Hall on the church grounds.

I also became involved in scouting again and became the Scout Master of Troop 45. Michael Nakatani had become the Scout Master of Troop 45 when Lanky became an executive on the Big Island and remained in that position until I returned to Maui. When the plantation started to phase out the camps, and the population began to shift to Central Maui, we moved to Kahului. I became the advisor for Explorer Post 101 of the Kahului Union Church for a number of years. I still traveled to Paia to continue as the Scout Master of Troop 45. My ties to Troop 45 were very sentimental, because I organized the troop in my high school days and enjoyed teaching the youngsters about the values of becoming good citizens and the educational information contained in the Boy Scout Handbook. When all the plantation camps were closed, Troop 45 did not exist anymore. However, it was revived for a few years when we formed Troop 45 with Maui Swim Club as the sponsor.

My association as a scoutmaster and adviser in the scouting role cannot come to a conclusion without the following refreshing inspirational dramas. The first narrative involved two brothers, Morris and Dennis Asato. Dennis, the younger brother, was athletically inclined, while the older brother, Morris was just the opposite. During a learn-to-swim class session at the Puunene Pool one evening, Morris just refused to let go of the gutter at the corner of the shallow end of the pool. While the other scouts were enjoying their swim across the pool, he continued to hug the gutter. After urging him several times to try to swim the length of the pool, I stepped back.

I am going ahead of the story, so will backtrack.

When I got married in March 1952, and before the European Armed Forces Swimming Championships scheduled for August in Berlin, Germany, I was admitted to the 97th General Hospital in Frankfurt for severe tonsillitis infection. After the usual treatment of my throat, the infection persisted for about a week.

I was then administered a series of injections around the clock. I was injected first on one arm, then the other, on the cheek of my butt, then the other cheek. Every few hours, different nurses would take turns, like a merry-go-round. I don't know if they enjoyed using me as a pin cushion. One evening, a nurse turned me over gently like a baby and inserted the needle into my numb butt and, after removing the needle, she patted my butt ever so soothingly, and I heard her melodious voice: "God bless you." I must have slept like a baby that night.

When the infection finally subsided, a young second lieutenant, who looked as if he had just graduated from medical school, took me into the operating room. I was apprehensive at first because of his youthful appearance, but after a few conversational exchanges with the doctor, I placed my health and welfare completely under his care. I think the young doctor had good practice and experience in removing my tonsils.

After my second week in the hospital, I prepared myself to swim in the championships in Berlin. I was in no condition to compete. I finished dead last in the 1500-m race, and when I lifted my head, there was a thunderous clapping of hands and yells, as if I had broken the world's record. I asked the swimmer who finished ahead of me what was going on. He said that the announcer kept repeating that I was the defending champion while I was swimming in my lane and even in my far-behind last performance, the audience cheered me. I never anticipated such a greeting.

Now back to my story about Morris and Dennis.

I kept on repeating that if he (Morris) did not attempt to swim the length of the pool, he would never know how good he is. I walked away, but kept the corner my eyes on him from the middle of the pool. I kept looking away, but from the corner of my eyes I was zeroed in on him. Morris kept looking around to see if anyone was watching him. Finally he started to stroke his way across the pool. He was struggling like a drowning swimmer, and my heart pounded like a sledgehammer.

When he finally negotiated the 25 yards, he turned his head, and there was a happy smile from ear to year. When I saw that satisfying smile from ear-to-ear, I felt like I was walking on air and all my effort and time in teaching the scouts how to swim were wrapped into a billion-dollar memorabilia chest. I don't think anybody saw him swim across the pool. I cheerfully floated over and congratulated him.

We entered a Boy Scout swimming meet at the Puunene Pool. I entered Morris in the 50-yard freestyle. He flatly refused to swim even before we went to the pool. I then told the members of Troop 45 about my experience in coming in last place in my race, and how I was cheered for finishing the race and for my effort.

Morris was built like a combination of a football linemen, weight-lifter and wrestler. He half jumped and half dove into the water and started his journey across the pool. He swam in lane five. If you ever saw a swimmer swim in a drowning-like manner in a competition, Morris would have been a perfect example. He kept on chugging along while the rest of the swimmers finished their 50-yard swim before Morris reached the 25-yard mark. On the way back to conclude his 50-yard race, the lifeguard kept walking on the side of the pool and motioned to me several times whether he should jump in to pull him out. I shook my head and motioned with my hands that he could finish the race.

It seemed like an hour for Morris to touch the 50-yard end. When Morris finally finished his grueling race, there was a deafening standing ovation that shook the ground and the water in the pool. The crowd didn't cheer Morris for coming in last place, but recognized and rattled the thunder from the sky for his Herculean effort!

The significance of the race was that not only can a winner be honored, but a last-place finisher can also receive showers of accolades for an all-out effort. Yes, I was elated and proud of Morris!

On the way back home, the scouts realized that what I mentioned about my last-place finish was not the essence of the story, but the importance of the effort you put in, that people, friends and parents really appreciate and honor any genuine effort. An excellent example was the memorable drowning-like swim of Morris.

I recall the swim of Morris because I met his brother Dennis at his parent's home in Kahului in July 2010, and after more than 50 years, we both remembered that race, and Dennis told me that he always relayed that story to his co-workers to emphasize the dignity of effort.

Dennis retired as an engineer from NASA, and Morris retired as a colonel from the U.S. Air Force.

The second anecdote involved two scouts on a camping trip to Manele Bay, Lanai, on July 26, 1999. There was a scout by the name of Terrance Suyama, son of scoutmaster Mervin Suyama of Troop 40. The other youth was Chad Horimoto of Troop 1. Troop 40 was sponsored by the Wailuku Hongwanji Church and Troop 1 sponsored by the Kahului Union Church. Scoutmaster Mervin was a former scout of Troop 45.

Terrance and the rest of the members of Troop 40 were enrolled in my swimming and life-saving merit badge classes at the Kahului Swimming Pool years ago. I do not know if Chad took any lessons, because there were so many classes by different troops in Maui County.

At the life-saving classes I repeatedly asserted that you never come in contact with a drowning person. You come in contact with a drowning person only as a last resort if you are qualified, and if you observe a drowning swimmer, you immediately take something with you to aid the victim.

In the heroic deed at Manele Bay, Terrance and Chad wisely took two boogie boards to a struggling father suffering with cramps in both his legs and his exhausted daughter and brought them safely to shore. They avoided direct contact with the victims as they were instructed in life-saving class. Scouts Terrance and Chad were honored with the Medal of Merit from the National Boy Scout office at a public gathering at the War Memorial Stadium.

These were tangible episodes, among many others, that my influence in my association with the Boy Scouts was fruitful.

In 1975, I received the Silver Beaver, the highest award given to a Scouter, from the Maui County Boy Scout Council, Boy Scouts of America. I was involved in the Boy Scout movement for over 60 years.

Boys of Scouting age should be involved in the Scouting movement sometime in their life. Not all of them will attain the rank of the highest achievement, the coveted Eagle Scout. However, as a young Scout and citizen, one is bound to learn something to enhance his life in some form.

My son, Spencer Jr., became an Eagle Scout as a member of Troop 1 of the Kahului Union Church, under Scoutmaster Stan Tadakuma. My 13-year-old grandson, Spencer E.P., recently became a member of Troop 1. Hopefully, he will continue the tradition of an Eagle Scout in the Shiraishi clan. Spencer Jr. is on the faculty at Maui Waena in Kahului, and my grandson is an eighth grader at Kamehameha Schools Maui campus at Pukalani.

The ladder of dreams and successes does not necessarily mean that one must or will finish at the top. There are different levels of successes. We all cannot become the president of the United States like Hawaii-born President Barack Obama. But we can all aspire to become the president of the United States, the most powerful man in the world. We all cannot become the president of a bank, a billionaire, a brain surgeon, a professor, a rocket scientist or a CEO of a large corporation. Somewhere on the ladder of dreams and successes, one will find a step that is suited for his or her vocation. And when that step is found according to his or her ambition and talent, one must pursue with vigor and expand that horizon to the utmost of the God-given gift.

The merit badge program for the Scouts offers various avenues of career choices, such as Agriculture, American Business, Astronomy, Animal Science, Architecture, Aviation, Engineering, Communications, Surveying, Soil and Water Conservation, and many, many more exciting selections.

Living in the plantation camps without the luxuries of toilet or shower facilities in the homes, no hot water, sharing beds with brothers or sisters, no refrigerator, no washing machine, no dryer, no telephones, hardly any privacy, low incomes and many negatives confronted by the plantation population, influenced a major desire for the younger generation to rise above the poverty level of their parents.

Today, a multitude of outstanding citizens have emerged from the plantation camps, such as politicians, judges, lawyers, teachers, doctors, principals, managers, business owners, coaches, scientists, athletes, outstanding citizens, dedicated volunteers etc., etc., etc.

If we look into the past of many of these outstanding citizens, we will see former Boy Scouts and Eagle Scouts. I believe the lessons learned through the Boy Scouts contributed greatly to their successes in adult life.

If only our parents were present with us now, they would be astonished beyond their wildest expectations at the accomplishments and successes of their offspring!

Age Group Swimming Begins

I became involved in the Maui Age Group swimming program sometime in the early 1960s when Alfred Deloso, who was the Deputy Director of Maui County Parks and Recreation Division, summoned three ordinary volunteer citizens to his office one day.

They were Lummy Pacheco, Benny Castor and Spencer Shiraishi.

Both Lummy and Benny are now sitting next to God and perhaps instructing the flying angels how to swim, just in case, heaven forbid, they accidentally fall into the ocean.

Lummy was a long-time county lifeguard who conducted learn-to-swim classes for the county. Benny was an established swimmer and coach of the Puunene Athletic Swim Club, and he was also the head coach of the Baldwin High School swimming team. In his youth, Benny swam in the Nationals under the legendary coach Soichi Sakamoto. Benny was a noteworthy breast stroker. Benny labored for Maui Electric Co. I was the lesser-known personality. Al Deloso called me because he knew that I was involved in teaching the Boy

Scouts how to swim and gave lifesaving lessons. Al and I had contacts many times because he came to the Maui Publishing Co. with sporting news that he gave to Wayne Tanaka, who was the sports editor of *The Maui News*. I was also an employee of the Maui Publishing Co.

When we met in Al's office in the War Memorial gym complex, he pointed out that Maui was once the proud powerhouse that dominated competitive swimming in the Islands, nationally and the world.

Since the dominating era of swimming by Duke Kahanamoku in three Olympics (Gold Medals in 1912 and 1920 and Silver in 1924 in the 100-meter freestyle) and the headliners of the past from Maui, competitive swimming on Maui was on the decline.

Al felt and believed that Maui could once again become the competitive force in swimming that it used to be when Coach Sakamoto was active on Maui. He proposed setting up a county swimming program with emphasis on recreational swimming to attract youngsters into the swimming atmosphere.

Perhaps a glimpse of the cherished and historical accomplishments by swimmers on Maui would shed light on the ambitious formation of the county's initial recreational age group swimming program.

Coach Sakamoto and his dedicated swimmers from Maui won the National Championships three consecutive years, 1939, 1940 and 1941. They all initially trained in an irrigation ditch before the Puunene Pool was built.

Prior to World War II in 1941, perhaps the majority of the population in the USA never heard of Pearl Harbor and never knew that Hawaii ever existed.

The aquatic world probably never heard of the island of Maui and the skinny teenage kids who splashed in the plantation irrigation ditch prior to their emergence as State, National and World dominating swimmers. And the unfamiliar name of Soichi Sakamoto was like an unpolished diamond hidden in the jungle of guava trees and sugar cane fields on an isolated island surrounded by water.

But the island of Maui became the focus of the world when the youngsters from the plantation camps began to shred State, National and World records. And the single man that was responsible for putting Maui on the world swimming map was none other than the tireless and fabled Coach Soichi Sakamoto. Coach Sakamoto later became a super-polished dazzling diamond among the top coaches in the world.

It started when the plantation luna (supervisor) on horseback continually harassed the kids swimming in the ditch in front of the Puunene School after school. It is reported that the youngsters used to swim in the nude, and when the luna chased them out of the ditch, they would run away in the nude through the school grounds, where Sakamoto was the science teacher. Sakamoto obtained permission from the plantation to let the teenagers swim in the ditch under his supervision.

Coach Sakamoto marked distances of 25 and 50 yards in large letters on the concrete sides of the ditch so that the swimmers could see how far they swam. They would relax and swim downstream, concentrating on their technique, and build strength when they resumed the struggle upstream again. This was repeated over and over, and the swimming world eventually adopted this "repetition" method of training.

Under Coach Sakamoto's persistent urging, the community-minded Hawaiian Commercial & Sugar Co. constructed a six-lane 25-yard swimming pool. After the construction of the pool, the swimmers who were accustomed to swim upstream against the current found that the water was so calm without any current that they felt like they were swimming downstream. The conditioned bodies of the swimmers made training easy in the pool that eventually rattled the swimming world when the initially irrigation-trained teenagers started to snap State, National and World records.

If the 1940 Olympics Games had been held in Helsinki, Sweden, as scheduled, we believe the majority of the USA Olympic swimmers could have been from Maui, swimmers like Bill Smith, Keo Nakama, Halo Hirose, Jose Balmores, Benny Castor, Bunny Nakama, Chick Miyamoto, Fujiko Katsutani, Mitsi Higuchi and Toyoko Tateyama

Unfortunately, the 1940 Olympics Games were canceled due to World War II. Only Bill Smith from the original field of great swimmers from Coach Sakamoto's rich treasury of talented champions ever competed in any Olympics. Bill captured the 1948 Olympic Gold in

London, England, in the 400-meter freestyle with new World and Olympic records. Bill also anchored the victorious USA 800-meter freestyle relay quartet in Olympic and World record times.

Many swimmers and coaches around the world came to Maui to train and to observe the dry-land exercises and the equipment used under Coach Soichi Sakamoto at the Puunene Pool. I even use some of his methods. Coach Sakamoto created his own sliding workout mechanism to strengthen the legs of the breast strokers, pulleys with weights to build upper body strength, and I witnessed Bill Smith toughen his flutter kick on a bench with chains shackled on each ankle.

Coach introduced the pink and blue cards for swimming meets to distinguish the gender when making entries. The pink card designated wahines, while the blue card was for kanes. The nation adopted the pink and blue cards as standard in all competitions until the introduction of the computer.

A number of USA national champions, like Jack Medica and Paul Herron, came to the Puunene Pool to train and compete with the Three Year Swim Club (3YSC) swimmers, notably against Bill Smith, Keo Nakama, Halo Hirose, Jose Balmores, to name a few, and National and World records were smashed during meets at that pool.

Even the Japanese Olympic team, headed by the world's 1,500-meter freestyle record-holder Furuhashi (nicknamed Flying Fish because he thrashed his arms and legs so fast that he appeared to be flying over the water) and teammate Hashizume trained and competed against the local sensations on their way to the 1948 Olympic Games in London, England.

The once-popular Puunene Pool, teeming with competitive swimmers, was located in the midst of the sugar cane field, isolated from the residential district. There were bleachers along the length of the 25-yard pool on the makai side and dressing rooms and showers for wahines and kanes at each end of the pool. A 10-foot diving board for diving competitions stood at the deep end of the pool, and a tall wooden fence wrapped around the pool and behind the bleachers made an appearance of a warm and cozy atmosphere.

Here are early members of the Three Year Swim Club (3YSC). Standing, left to right, are Coach Soichi Sakamoto, Mike Ginoza, John Tsukano, Halo Hirose, Takeshi Kit-agawa, Bill Neunzig, Bull Yoshina, Charlie Oda, Pundy Yokouchi, Benny Castor, Mr. Takayama and Coach's brother, Bill Sakamoto. In the middle row, left to right, are Hiroshi Shigetani, Yoshio Shibuya, Jose Balmores, Bunmei Nakama, Keo Nakama, Tommy Yamashita and Mac Nakano. In the bottom row, left to right, are Chick Miyamoto, Kay Sugano, Lulu Nakagawa, Toyoko Takeyama, Doris Yoshino, Natalie Sato, Mitzie Higuchi and Fujiko Katsutani. Thanks to Mitzie Higuchi for helping to identify everyone.

Besides the swimming pool there were tennis courts, a football field and a baseball diamond with bleachers. All the sporting activities were in a concentrated area that made it convenient for the participants and the spectators.

Most of the heralded swimmers hailed from Puunene's Camp 5 Village, which was at the crossroads corner between the school and the pool. The Kahului Railroad Co.'s bus line terminated at Camp 5 Store before heading back to the main station in Kahului, and many swimmers stopped at the store on their way to or from practice.

When the population of the plantation camps shifted elsewhere and the camps were no more, the pool was neglected. Instead of hosting national-caliber swimming competitions, the pool was utilized to raise catfish. The pool is still in existence today, August 6, 2010. The tennis courts and the playing fields are no longer to be seen.

About 10 years ago, when Bill Smith came to honor Coach Sakamoto at the Coach Sakamoto Invitational, Wayne Tanaka and I accompanied Bill to the Puunene Pool. Bill wanted to go on a nostalgic trip to the pool where he spent oodles of strenuous hours training under Coach Sakamoto to accomplish his amazing feats in smashing NCAA, National, World and Olympic records.

When we went there, Bill was saddened to see the pool in such a deplorable condition. The shallow end of the pool was dry. At the deep end of the pool were water hyacinths, perhaps with catfish frolicking underneath.

Bill Smith and I look over the abandoned Puunene Pool.

I went to the pool on August 6, 2010, just to check on its condition, because I was writing about the Puunene Pool in a small way. I peered through the chain-link fence and noticed that the water hyacinths were gone at the deep end of the pool. In their place were three turtles swimming in the brackish water polluted with rubbish. There were three brown-colored ducks sunning themselves on the mauka side of the dry concrete about the middle of the pool and a pair of black-and-white-feathered ducks and a pig in an open enclosure at the eastern dry corner of the shallow end of the once proud and productive pool of champions.

If Bill Smith ever saw what I perceived, Bill would have automatically and reverentially whispered with tears in his eyes towards heaven, "Coach, what have they done to your precious pool?"

With its rich history of triumphant performances by the local mermen and mermaids at the Puunene Pool, statewide, nationally and around the globe, it is a sad and sobbing ending of the Puunene Swimming Pool, the birth place of State, National, World and Olympic heroes of the past from Maui.

Perhaps a person with a sky-high miraculous power and an ocean-deep influence may boldly step forward to the front line to ignite a sentimental rocket that may lead to the restoration of the former pride and joy of the swimming community on Maui and in the state.

Coach Sakamoto accepted a faculty position with the University of Hawaii after World War II and was the head swimming coach of the University until his retirement from the Manoa staff in 1971. Coach Sakamoto's departure created a Haleakala-crater-size vacuum in the swimming circle on Maui.

Al Deloso wanted us to help get competitive swimming started again by first teaching youngsters to swim in a recreational program. The only veteran and active coach in the 1950s and early 1960s was Benny Castor, head coach of Baldwin High School and the age group swimming club of the Puunene Athletic Club. Benny and his club traveled to Honolulu for swim competitions many times. Under Al's plan, Benny would continue to use the swimming pool next to the sugar mill. Lummy Pachecho was assigned the old four-lane-by-25-yard swimming pool in Wailuku, and her team was named the Wailuku Swim Club. I was given the six-lane-by-25-yard Kahului Pool to organize a recreational swimming program. We called ourselves the Kahului Swim Club.

When the youngsters became proficient in swimming after the introduction of the recreational phase, the county began to introduce beginners' swimming competition. The distance was mostly 25 and 50 yards. It was fun watching the fledgling youngsters compete. Eventually, the distances of the events were increased to 50, 100, 200 and 500 yards in the freestyle and to 50, 100 and 200 yards in the other strokes, and relays were introduced. But the 25-yard events remained for the eight-and-under and beginner swimmers.

That was the beginning of the age-group swimming on Maui. The County's dreams and hopes of the recreational and competitive age-group programs have since mushroomed from a trio of clubs into a successful streamlined alliance of six clubs. The six clubs joined hands and called themselves MAGSA (Maui Age Group Swimming Association). The president and the officers of the association are rotated among the clubs. There are no dues in the association. MAGSA owes a million dollars worth of gratitude to the mayors, Board of Supervisors, councilwomen and councilmen of Maui County, past and present, for their untold support the County has provided to swimming and other sports on Maui.

I have expressed many, many times to coaches and officials on the outer islands that Maui County is the best county in the state!

However, before we became the smooth operation of MAGSA as we know today, there were a multitude of tickling and irritating circumstances in the past that merit to be unfolded.

The majority of the County meets were held at the Puunene Pool. Others were held at the old Wailuku Pool before the War Memorial 50-meter swimming pool was constructed.

At one point, the County provided medals to individual swimmers and outstanding trophies to performers in each age division after the swimming season. Medals and trophies were awarded during potlucks at the clubhouse next to the pool by the mill. I felt at that time it was a wonderful gesture on the part of Maui County Department of Parks and Recreation to honor the swimmers.

However, some of the coaches and parents did not see eye-to-eye about the County's selection of the outstanding swimmers. After the continued grievances, the County decided that it was not worth the troublesome encounters and discontinued the potluck gatherings and presentation of medals and trophies.

With only three clubs in the formative stage of swimming, it was rather easy to submit our entries to the person who made the entries on paper. The swimming events, times and the names of the swimmers were typewritten, and the clubs were furnished 8½-by-14-inch mimeographed sheets, known today as psych sheets. The tedious job of typing the entries and making copies were handled by Ross Tamayose of the County, who is now happily retired.

Today, in the year of 2010, everything is done by computer, which makes it easier, cleaner and faster. The computer handles hundreds of entries in minutes.

At one of the final swim meets, perhaps in 1968, we submitted our entries. Maui Swim Club outnumbered the swimmers from the other two clubs combined. After the entries were submitted, all the coaches met. I was told by the other coaches that if our swimmers were entered in an event and if there was no other swimmer entered from another club, our swimmers could not swim. I felt that was truly unfair, just because we had a larger number of swimmers. The other coaches persisted.

The following day I went to see Nolle Smith, the Parks Director. Nolle was a roommate of Mayor Hannibal Tavares at UH and was a football all-star. I told Nolle what had transpired. He felt the same way I did. He then informed the other coaches that the County could not go along with their decision. I also called Coach Sakamoto about our situation and asked for his opinion. Coach replied, "More power to a big club."

There were minor County interferences, a coach criticizing a volunteer official, coaches not adhering to the rules, swimmers transferring from club to club and returning to the original club, petty jealousies, and so on.

In one instance, two swimmers from another club came to the Kahului Pool after training with their regular club several times and asked yours truly to teach them the flip turn. I did not tell them to come. When their coach found out what they were doing, they were suspended for two weeks. In another case, there was an excellent breast stroker at one of the high schools, who was one of the three top qualifiers in the State the previous year. He came to the Kahului Pool without my urging to train during the summer. He continued to train with Maui Swim Club in September. He was kicked out of his high school team after the coach learned of his whereabouts. When I found out what had happened, I told the swimmer to approach the coach and to apologize. He emphatically asserted that he did not want to crawl on his hands and knees. So he did not swim his senior year. I called his coach to inform him that the swimmer came on his own to train with me. I asked him to forgive and let the student swim, to no avail.

Yes, we encountered growing pains, but they were hurdled into a brighter future.

Maui Grows New Swim Champs

Because the Puunene Athletic Swimming Club had been in existence since the 1950s, the early county swimming-meet encounters were dominated by its members. We watched in awe as its swimmers plastered all the other competitors. It was a one-sided affair. The team scores were outrageously lopsided, a difference of more than 1,000 points from first place to the second place.

Our club started off with about 12 swimmers who stuck together after the recreational phase of the program. We swam twice a week. The other clubs had a five-day training cycle. Our swimmers were hammered by the other clubs, so we started to train three days a week. Our swimmers were still being clobbered by the other swimmers, so we initiated a five-day training schedule. Our swimmers began to improve and gradually became equal to the other swimmers. As time went by, the membership of Kahului Swim Club began to grow rapidly. We gradually started to gain ground. And we began to outscore our opponents by more than 1,000 points. We continued to spread the team points. At one point, the other coaches suggested that we not keep team scores. I agreed, and from that moment, we did not keep scores at the County meets. And up to 2010, we haven't kept team scores at all the County swim meets.

Our swimmers began to finish first in many individual events and to break county records. Our membership grew, and we became the largest age group club on Maui.

We started to go to off-island swimming meets, and the swimmers in Honolulu repeatedly kept asking: "Where is Kahului?" So we changed our name to Maui Swim Club.

Many outstanding swimmers were developed from the clubs on Maui. The Hawaiian swimming record book was loaded and is still engraved with names like Matthew Cerizo, Kaina Awai, Kaimana Apo, Keith Shirota, Cheyne Block, Caleb Rowe, Kristen Nagata, Chelsea Nagata, Randall Tom, Neil Ichiki, Curtis Hirai, Tami Hondo, Shari Irimata, Christine Hayashi, Reece Kaya, Ailani Miller, Ilima Mahoney, Kalani Rosell, Troy Kojenlang, Darin Irimata, Tyson Matsui, Jason Matsui, Michael Nishimitsu, Jason Creelman, Akiko Uyeda, Libby Matthews, Renny Richmond and others.

While a senior at St. Anthony in 1986 and a member of Maui Swim Club, Matthew Cerizo owned all the boys' Maui Interscholastic League (MIL) swimming records. Kim Takamori, also of Maui Swim Club, while a senior at Maui High School in 1991 became the first wahine swimmer to ink her name in the record book for every record in the MIL girl's division.

The super performances of Matthew and Kim have never been duplicated since.

Matthew, as a 12-year-old performer in 1981, was credited with 10 Hawaiian records in a single season. Kim, as a 17-18 age division competitor, won all 12 individual events in the 1991 State Championships. That was the first time ever in the history of swimming in the State that a swimmer won all the individual events.

Matthew obtained a full swimming scholarship at Texas A&M and is now an agent for the Allstate Insurance Co. in Kihei. Matthew is married to Serena, from a prominent family from Manila, and has two sons. Dr. Kim has become a respected optometrist at the Kaiser Medical Clinic in Wailuku, is married to Kyle Ginoza and has two daughters.

Chelsea Nagata and Randall Tom pose with me at the pool.

Chelsea Nagata, of Maui Swim Club, while an eighth grader at Maui Waena School in Kahului, became the youngest swimmer in the State to qualify for the Junior Nationals. Chelsea, with her sister Kristen, parents Noreen and Andrew and I, traveled to Anchorage, Alaska, for the Junior Nationals.

Chelsea, along with Randall Tom of Maui Swim Club and HSC's Caleb Rowe and Cheyne Block, qualified for the 2008 USA Olympic trials at Omaha, Nebraska. Randall placed ninth in the 100-meter butterfly in the Olympic trials. A commendable performance. Kristen Nagata qualified for the Olympic trials in 2004. Proud feathers for them to wear.

Randall represented the USA as a member of the National Team that participated in the World Championships in London, England in 2006.

Chelsea was named an NCAA All-American as a scholar swimmer with an eighth place finish in the NCAA finals while a student at University of California, Irvine.

An up-and-coming blooming youngster named Jonah Hu, of Maui Swim Club, smashed 10 out of 12 Maui County short-course records in the 11-12 age-group division in 2009.

Fred Haywood, a product of the Puunene Athletic Swim Club, went to the Mainland to train along with Mark Spitz of Olympic fame. Fred became the NCAA king in the backstroke and was credited as the world windsurfing champion. Fred was inducted into the Hawaiian Swimming Hall of Fame and was invited to say a few words of encouragement and advice to members of Maui Swim Club one afternoon.

A bundle of swimmers from Maui have earned full swimming scholarships at various universities and colleges, much to the delight of their parents.

In the early days of swimming in the state, there were no mandatory registration and liability fees. Also, there were no entry fees, and no individual qualifying times were required to enter a swimming meet. Today, every swimmer must register, with a mandatory payment of $62 per year. The bulk of the registration fee goes to the USA Swimming Committee in Colorado Springs, Colorado, and a small percentage to the Hawaii Local Swim Committee. The local clubs do not receive a share of the registration fee. Today, if a swimmer wants to enter a swim meet, there are fees for an individual event that range from $2 to $3, depending on the type of competition.

When the fee and entry requirements came into place, Maui Swim Club's first "AA" swimmer was Ann Murayama (Mrs. Dennis Irimata). Ann swam in her first competition in Honolulu in the prestigious Keo Nakama Invitational.

Maui Swim Club's initial State champion was 14-year-old Jocelyn Romero (Mrs. Mustafa Dermirbag) in the 100-yard breast stroke in the 13-14 age bracket at the Kamehameha High School pool on Oahu. Jocelyn was asthmatic and had to use an inhaler between our sprint training sessions. Fortunately, she has since outgrown her discomfort. Jocelyn's daughter, Angelina, followed her mother's swim strokes by capturing the 10-and-under age division in the 50 and 100-meter breast stroke State titles at the Barber's Point swimming pool. Jocelyn was followed by a host of State champs and recorder holders.

Maui's Pools

When we first organized, the swimming pool next to the sugar mill was used by members of the Puunene Athletic Club Swimming Club, who were primarily haoles, so it was called the haole pool. There also was a social hall with kitchen facilities next to the pool on Puunene Avenue. The social hall was utilized many times by the American Red Cross to conduct first aid classes, and that is where I received my first aid instructor's certificate. The County also hosted several age group swimming potluck gatherings and award ceremonies in the club house.

There were no heaters at the pools way back then. The temperature of the water ranged from the high 60s to the low 70s. Swimmers endured the cold and the wind, and we were still able to produce state champions and record holders. The Kahului Pool was fenced with chain link around the pool. The pool was elevated, and whenever a strong wind came from northeast, it swept through the fence and made the swimmers shiver. I asked Parks Director Poison Inouye if the County could put some kind of a protective cover over the chain-link fence to keep the wind out. He said that he could do better. The County installed a hollow-tile wall on the Paia side, to the joy and happiness of the swimmers and parents.

Also, whenever a kona wind was generated, the wind would roar through the fence like a tornado from the Wailuku side. When the pipes and the wire fence became corroded, it started to become hazardous for the swimmers.

Alan Arakawa, then the County Council Parks Committee Chairman, spearheaded additional improvements at the Kahului Pool. A hollow-tile wall and a roof were installed, and the parking lot was extended and paved. Much mahalo to Alan. Alan became the Maui County mayor later.

Since the water was so cold during the winter months, we were afraid that the youngsters might become sick. Members of Maui Swim Club huddled together one day with a private solar-water-heater installer, and he came up with the cost and the number of solar panels required to provide warm water for the Kahului Pool. We presented the proposition to the Parks Department, with the stipulation that if our

92

proposition were accepted, our club members would provide the necessary manpower.

After closely scrutinizing the cost factor of the solar panels versus the electric water heater, the Parks Department sided with the electric heater. The Parks Department said that the initial cost of the solar panels was too high compared to the electric system. The private solar installer agreed that the initial cost was much higher than the electric heater, but he said that in time the cost factor would even out and in the long term, would become cheaper than electric.

With today's oil price, the cost for the electric water heater must be higher than the Iao Needle in the West Maui Mountains.

Today, swim competitors in Maui County are enjoying the comfort of training in heated pools with hot showers. Not only the competitive swimmers have the benefit of the heated pools and hot showers; they are also shared by the public, learn-to-swim youngsters, aerobics classes, masters and lap swimmers.

We are mighty proud and fortunate that we have had, and continue to have, wonderful concerned politicians and mayors that always look after the welfare of the citizens.

About 45 years ago, we took around 20 swimmers to compete in the National Junior Olympics at the Farrington High School swimming pool. It was a 50-meter pool, and there was a diving well separated from the pool.

That was the first time our swimmers from Maui ever saw such a l-----o-----n-----g pool. Their first reaction was: "You mean we have to swim that far?" Ah, yes, it was a daunting feat to negotiate 50 meters, especially since Maui did not have a 50-meter pool.

Upon our return after our swimmers' grueling introduction to competing in a 50-meter pool, I talked to Wayne Tanaka, sports editor of *The Maui News*. I told him that the swimmers on Maui were at a disadvantage against swimmers on Oahu because we trained and competed in only 25-yard pools.

The story appeared in *The Maui News* sports section, and that started the movement for a 50-meter pool on Maui. I testified numerous times at the Board of Supervisors meetings and at committee gatherings in the evenings.

Fujio (Bear) Sone was the parks director and Sheik Kono the lifeguard supervisor. Members of the Board of Supervisors were, if memory serves me right, Hannibal Tavares, Rick Medina, Goro Hokama, Manuel Molina, Joe Bulgo, Toshi Anzai, Richard Caldito and Marco Meyer.

Our mayor then was the gung-ho type Eddie Tam.

After many revisions and discussions, plans for the 50-meter pool were finally approved in 1968. Fuku (Fukunaga) Construction Co. was awarded the contract to build the pool next to the Memorial Gym and did an outstanding piece of work without any flaws.

I was at ease at the Kahului Swimming Pool (previously known as the Salvation Army Swimming Pool) because I was a part of the volunteer work crew that built the pool on weekends. Engineers, carpenters, draftsmen, businessmen and ordinary citizens from the Dream City area donated their time and expertise every weekend. It was a community-built pool.

There were humorous and informative incidents in the then Mayor Hannibal Tavares's office many, many years ago. When the subject of a new swimming pool to be built in Lahaina emerged, Mayor Tavares objected to that idea. I went to see the mayor in the hopes that he might be persuaded to side with the people of Lahaina for a new pool.

When I mentioned the benefits to be derived by the citizens of Lahaina and the hotels and a boost to Maui's economy by constructing the pool, the mayor said: "Why can't the people in Lahaina build a pool like the people did in Kahului."

It was a pleasant shock when the mayor said that. I told him that I was one of the multitude of volunteers to whom he was referring. He commented that he was also a working volunteer, even though he did not live in Dream City. Perhaps we were working side-by-side and didn't even know it. The mayor added that he enjoyed working on weekends as a volunteer at the Kahului Swimming Pool because the wives of the workers provided ono kau kau for lunch. Amen to that. No offense to Mrs. Tavares' cooking.

Tavares at that time was the personnel director for the HC&S Co., with his office at the Puunene Swimming Pool. I saw him several times when we competed with 3YSC at the pool, but I didn't know who he was.

While I was in Mayor Tavares' office, we covered several items not related to politics. Among other items of mutual interest, I learned that he was one of the top runners in the state while a student at Farrington High School, where he excelled in the 440-yard race. He trained by running on the hills in the Kalihi area. Those who knew Tavares when he was a member of the Board of Supervisors and the mayor of Maui County would never in their wildest dreams think that he was once a track star, because of his size. In his later years, he resembled more like a sumotori. He also mentioned that when he was an instructor at Maui High School, he attended football games because he enjoyed watching my sister, Jane, perform as a song leader. My sister must have been very attractive in her youth at Maui High School, because she was chosen as the Junior Prom Queen for the Junior Prom festivities.

It was a joy and a pleasure to have easy access to our friendly Mayor Hannibal Tavares.

When the retired mayor became ill and was a patient at the Straub Clinic on Oahu, I took a bunch of our young swimmers after a swim meet to the clinic to cheer the mayor. We went upstairs to his room. Mrs. Tavares was at the door of the room. I asked her if we could see the mayor and perhaps he would be happy to see the smiling faces of the youngsters from Maui. She didn't know who I was. When I told her my name was Spencer Shiraishi, her face lit up--perhaps she recognized my name--and went into the room to inform the mayor that he had visitors from Maui. The mayor recognized me immediately and told us to come in.

The mayor didn't look his usual self, and yet he welcomed the swimmers and me into his room. We made the visit short. I was exceedingly happy to have visited him with our swimmers, and perhaps he felt the same way. We wished our mayor well and a speedy recovery. Our mayor recovered fully and returned to Maui.

When Governor Linda Lingle was the mayor of Maui County, she pushed for pools in Lahaina, Kihei and Pukalani. Gov. Lingle was a dedicated and accomplished swimmer and swam with the masters swimming club in the evenings at the Maui Memorial Pool (Coach Soichi Sakamoto Swimming Pool). All the swimmers, parents and coaches are grateful to her.

Our present mayor, Charmaine Tavares, was the parks director when her father was the mayor and the subject of the Lahaina pool emerged. I went to the Lahaina Civic Center for a hearing about the new pool in Lahaina. I testified in favor of the pool and made a comment that with the pleasant weather in Lahaina 365 days of the year, Lahaina could develop into the mecca of swimming in Hawaii. Charmaine Tavares was also at the gathering. As we understand, our Mayor Charmaine took swimming lessons under Coach Sakamoto while a student at UH.

There were no electronic timing devices in the entire state. When I read about the futuristic advantages the Colorado Timing electronic scoreboard provided, I went to the Board of Supervisors to ask if Maui County could possibly purchase one.

I was referred to the Finance Committee. I gathered whatever cost factor information necessary from the Colorado Timing device company and made my presentation. The Finance Committee was very cordial and thanked me for the information on the cost and benefits of the electronic timing scoreboard.

The Finance Committee approved the request and it was OK'd by the Board of Supervisors. Maui County was the first in the State to purchase an electronic scoreboard, even before the Duke Kahanamoku swimming complex at the UH.

The electronic scoreboard was on wheels and was utilized at the deep end of the pool under the shady area. The scoreboard became a huge hit with the swimmers, parents, fans and officials, because they were able to see the times and the places of the swimmers instantly, one at a time.

With my electronics background, I maintained the electronic device without pay, usually during my lunch breaks and on weekends.

When Marilyn Kahoohanohano was the parks director, we took the electronic scoreboard to a track meet as an experiment, and the runners and fans enjoyed viewing the times instantly.

After a tenure as parks director under Mayor Hannibal Tavares, Marilyn accepted a position in the athletic department at UH, where she is still active.

After several years, John Buck of the Parks Division recommended to the parks director to purchase a full compliment of eight scoreboards. When the request was granted, Maui County was again the first in the state to install an eight-electronic-scoreboards configuration. The impressive system enabled the swimmers, parents, fans and officials to view instant results of the eight swimmers.

At one of the County swim meets, a swimmer from Maui Swim Club, Pat Tobin, shattered a Hawaiian record in the 100-meter breast stroke event in the 13-14 age division. We submitted the record to the Hawaii Local Swim Committee to be recognized as a new Hawaiian record, but it was denied because Maui did not have an official referee.

I promptly went to see our Mayor Hannibal Tavares and informed him of the unfortunate rejection of the Hawaiian record and solicited his kokua in solving the situation by obtaining a referee, since it was a county program. The mayor immediately started the ball rolling to have two county officials certified as referees. I suggested that the referees should come from the ranks of the county because of their potential longevity. Al Deloso thought otherwise. He wanted to have a swimmer's parent become a referee. I responded that it would be fine if a parent had youngsters who continued swimming. Then the parent would probably stay to officiate as a referee. I cited an example of a parent who returned to Maui with his sons, and he had been active as an official in Honolulu. He would have been an excellent choice to become a referee. However, when his sons left swimming, the father also became inactive, and I thought that probably would happen with parent referees.

John Buck and Stanley Nako, both county Parks employees, were selected.

According to the rules and regulations, they were required to go to Honolulu to work side by side with a certified referee. They also worked with referees who would come to work in the Maui County meets. Whenever we went to swim meets in Honolulu, the county paid their plane fare, and John, Stanley and I would sleep on the floor in our sleeping bags with the rest of our swimmers in a single room.

Today most of our referees and officials are parents who have their children in swimming clubs. Some have dropped out when their children left the swimming scene. We sincerely hope that our present crop of officials will continue in their official capacities. MAGSA has continually attempted to recruit parents to become involved with their youngsters as officials at swim meets.

Presently, in 2010, the clubs on Maui are the Lahaina Swim Club, coached by Tom Popdan; in Kihei, the South Maui Sharks, coached by Janet Renner; in Pukalani, the Maui Dolphins, coached by Malcom Cooper; in Wailuku, the Hawaii Swimming Club, coached by Reid Yamamoto; in Kahului, the Maui Gold, coached by Ray and son Tyler Orikasa, and the Maui Swim Club, coached by Spencer Shiraishi. Each club has its own training facility. At one time, before Lahaina, Kihei, Pukalani and Maui Gold came into the picture, there was a club at Seabury Hall School, headed by Mrs. Charlotte Melrose. Mrs. Melrose's husband was the headmaster of Seabury Hall. When Mrs. Melrose left Maui, the Seabury Hall team folded.

Before the South Maui Sharks were organized, a swimming-consulting-type of person from the Mainland was on Maui on a vacation. He displayed interest in swimming in Kihei and was scheduled to meet with the parents. Before he made his recommendation, a parent of the forming Sharks club called, and I mentioned that perhaps all the clubs on Maui should congregate together and call ourselves the Maui Aquatic Club or Team. Also, the head coach could be rotated among the clubs on Maui. She thought that it was a wonderful thought. At the meeting with the consulting-type of adviser, the parents of the future Maui Sharks were advised that it would be beneficial if all the clubs would become one to form a championship team for the welfare of Maui County. His line of thinking was in tune with mine.

Unfortunately, the vision of one club on Maui fell by the wayside.

Along came Chuck Uyeda, who founded the Maui No Ka Oi Swim Club. Chuck organized No Ka Oi with about 10 polished swimmers who defected from Maui Swim Club. Chuck had a daughter, Akiko, who rose from the Maui Swim Club's learn-to-swim program to rule the 10-Under age division in the State.

Akiko was like a well-oiled machine and endured the cold water and the repeated hard training with the older accomplished swimmers. Chuck would sit by the entrance of the pool. Whenever I felt that Akiko had enough training, I told her to go home. When Akiko went to the gate, Chuck would send her back to continue training. Akiko was obedient and did not complain that she was cold and tired. Chuck confided in me one day, saying that he liked the way we trained and whenever his daughter would come home, he would jot down whatever she practiced. Before Chuck decided to form his own club, he said that perhaps Maui Swim Club could win the Coach Sakamoto Invitational. His prediction came true because Maui Swim Club won the Coach Sakamoto Invitational for five consecutive years.

No Ka Oi later fused with the Hawaii Swimming Club organization, the main body in Honolulu. The joint venture survived a short time. When No Ka Oi was no more, a new club with its former members was formed as the Maui Gold Swim Team, under the capable guidance of John Nakano.

One year I became discouraged with the age-group program because our swimmers did not continue their swimming in high school. I felt that the youngsters were wasting their time and valuable home-work studies.

I dropped out of the program for about a year. Upon the urging of the parents and by my boss, Mrs. Nora Cooper, I returned with re-newed vigor before the year was out.

During my absence, Ed Tamura organized a team from members of the Maui Swim Club who attended St. Anthony and called themselves the Kahului Aquatic Team (KAT). Ed was employed by Aloha Airlines and became the head coach of St. Anthony High School. KAT joined with two other clubs on Oahu and the Big Island to organize a formidable four-team Aloha Aquatic Association (AAA). The AAA took full control of the competitive swimming in the State, especially the relays, for several years.

The glimmer of AAA started to dim when the Maui AAA members left the association.

The remainder of the former AAA swimmers became members of the Hawaii Swimming Club (HSC). Reid Yamamoto, who swam for the University of Hawaii team and the Hawaii Swimming Club under Coach Sakamoto in Honolulu, became the head coach of the local club. Reid later married a Maui wahine and had a daughter. Reid was a member of Maui County lifeguard crew at the Memorial Pool. Currently he is a member of the Maui High School faculty and is the swimming head coach of the Sabers.

When the AAA dominance flickered, a new merger emerged with clubs from Oahu, Molokai, the Big Island and Maui under the banner of the Hawaii Swimming Club. The fearsome four-island aggregation commenced to cement all competitions in the State, just as AAA did in its prime.

HSC swam rough-shod over all competition and continued to reap swimming headlines for years. After the glory-filled-years, HSC's sparkling flares started to sputter, and it became just a shadow of its former status.

Maui Swim Club, organized by home-grown swimmers, stole some fire from HSC by capturing the State Championships in 1991 and in 1993. It was the first time ever for a club from outside of Oahu to garner the Hawaiian championship. The last time Maui enjoyed a championship year was under Coach Sakamoto with the 3YSC in 1941. In 1991, the Maui Swim Club, besides garnering the State title, won almost every major invitational swimming meet, the Kamehameha, Manoa, Pearl City and the Coach Sakamoto Invitationals. The Aulea Invitational was the only competition that escaped Maui Swim Club's onslaught, because a huge contingent of about 60 swimmers from Japan prevented a clean sweep.

The history of swimming or any other sporting activity on Maui cannot ignore the everyday-ready-to-help-seven-day-twenty-fours-a-day contributions of Kenji Kawaguchi. In his prime at Lahainaluna, Kenji was an all-star football, basketball and track performer.

While the deputy director under Marilyn in the Parks Department, Kenji encouraged the county part-time workers to be timers at all the County swim meets. In those days when Kenji was active, the parents were able to sit in the bleachers and enjoy their potential swimming champs perform. Today, all the parents are required to take turns to become timers and officials.

When we first started our invasion of Oahu, we were totally lost as to the different location of the pools, where to catch the bus, where to transfer and how much. We ended up returning to our hotel very late in the evenings.

In the early days of competition, the swimming meets dragged on for six to nine hours a day. That was extremely tiring and demanding for the swimmers, parents and the officials.

About 2007, the National Governing Board on Age Group Swimming at Colorado Springs, Colorado, came up with the recommendation that all competitions involving 12-and-under age swimmers should not exceed four hours. That was a wise and humane decision.

Al Deloso's determination and ambition to revive swimming on Maui from recreational to competitive levels have flourished to the point where Maui can now compete on equal terms with the other clubs in the state. And many have competed and are still competing in college level. Maui should be grateful and proud of the efforts of Al. Thank you, Al Deloso.

Al was killed, along with four others, in a plane crash in November of 1996 on Molokai on their return flight to Maui after a political rally.

Honoring Coach Sakamoto

Swimming in Hawaii owes a great deal to Coach Soichi Sakamoto. One evening many years ago, the Hawaiian Swimming Coaches Association met at the Primo Beer Brewing Company's conference room in Honolulu and adopted a resolution to name the new University of Hawaii swimming pool complex "Coach Soichi Sakamoto Swimming Pool," in honor of Coach Sakamoto. I was the only coach from Maui in attendance at the gathering, and I signed the resolution. Ralph Goto, coach of the Windward Y Swim Club, was the driving force. The attempted resolution to name the University complex in honor of Coach Sakamoto did not fare well, as the name of former Olympic champion

Duke Kahanamoku was selected by the higher-up pool nominating committee.

All the coaches were disappointed when Coach Sakamoto's name was not chosen. We felt that Coach Sakamoto had direct connections with the UH as a faculty member and as the coach of the UH swimming team.

However, we cannot deny the legacy of Duke Kahanamoku. Duke was an Olympic champion, a world-renowned celebrity, an unofficial good-will ambassador of Hawaii, a former sheriff of Honolulu, a surfing sensation who possessed an explosive smiling personality that captivated everyone he came in contact with.

When Wayne Tanaka was the president of Maui Swim Club many, many years ago, I brought up the subject of sponsoring the Coach Soichi Sakamoto Invitational. The thought of sponsoring the invitational had been in the back of my head for years, but I felt that our club did not have the numbers to undertake the monumental task of sponsoring an invitational.

Wayne had three children in the club. Wayne and I thought that the time was ripe because our club now had the numbers. But first we had to ask Coach Sakamoto for his permission to use his illustrious name.

When I approached Coach to ask if it were OK to sponsor a meet with his name, he was happy and answered: "I would be honored."

In 1975, the inaugural Coach Sakamoto Invitational was held. The year of 2010 was the 36th Annual Coach Sakamoto Memorial Invitational Swimming Meet. The Coach Sakamoto Invitational is the only major swimming meet outside of Oahu and is the third-longest running major invitational in the state.

Coach Sakamoto passed away August 2, 1997, at the age of 91. The War Memorial Swimming Pool was dedicated and re-named the Coach Soichi Sakamoto Swimming Pool as an honor and a living memorial later that year. Alan Shishido, then deputy director under Director Charmaine Tavares, led the charge in dedicating the pool in recognition of Coach Sakamoto.

I stand with Coach Soichi Sakamoto to display his award at the annual invitational meet named for him.

International Connections

When the USA boycotted the 1980 Olympic Games in Russia, Maui Swim Club invited Coach Don Gambril, head coach of University of Alabama, and two of his would-have-been Olympic swimmers to the Coach Sakamoto Invitational. Coach Gambril was an assistant coach of the 1980 Olympic Team. He became the head coach of the USA Olympic swimming team in 1984, held at Los Angeles.

Coach Gambril and Coach Sakamoto were close friends, and Coach Gambril was familiar with the exploits of Bill Smith, Keo Nakama, Halo Hirose, Bunny Nakama, Jose Balmores and others of fame who were developed by Coach Sakamoto.

There were intriguing stories about my association with Coach Gambril. When he was here for the Coach Sakamoto Invitational, he conducted a swimming clinic with his swimmers to anyone who was interested. He also noticed the swimming talent and capabilities of 11-year-old Matthew Cerizo. He asked that he be kept informed about Matthew's progress. During Matthew's senior year at St. Anthony, he snapped the Hawaii high school 100-yard butterfly record. After his

103

superb swim, we flew to Orlando, Florida to compete in the Senior National Championships. He finished tenth overall. Matthew and I were invited by Coach Gambril to visit the campus of the University of Alabama after the Senior Nationals.

Coach Gambril with Wilma and me on a visit to Maui in 1991.

Coach Gambril wanted Matthew to become a Crimson Tide swimmer. However, somewhere along the path of selecting an educational institution, Matthew decided to pursue his swimming and educational careers at Texas A&M.

There is a jovial advisory comment that I usually reserve to the high school graduates and older swimmers who plan to continue their higher education on the Mainland: "If you want to marry a millionaire, go to New York or Texas." Perhaps Matthew remembered my voice deep inside the cavity of his head, and that directed him to Texas. Did Matthew marry a millionaire from Texas? Nope. But he did marry a millionaire's daughter... from Manila!

After the 1984 Olympic Games, I wrote to Coach Gambril that I was taking my family to Germany in October, and that I was planning to visit the training site of Michael Gross, the former Olympic and World record-holder in the 100 and 200 meter butterfly.

Coach Gambril did not waste any time in replying. He wrote saying that if I saw Gross, to tell him that he could enjoy a full ride at the

University of Alabama. Evidently, Coach Gambil wanted to add Gross to his arsenal.

In Germany I informed my sister-in-law and her husband that I would like to visit the training site of Michael Gross. They immediately tossed their arms up and declared that it would be next to impossible to see him, because he was isolated and protected by his mother from the press and visitors.

I patiently said, let's give it a try. It was about a 20-minute drive from the town of Fechenheim, where my wife had lived, to the pool in Offenbach where Gross trained.

At the pool, there was an elongated covered tunnel leading to the main entrance of the 50-meter pool. There was a lovely middle-aged lady at the entrance, perhaps to control people going into the pool.

I asked in English if Michael Gross was training here. She said, "Yes." I told her that my name was Spencer Shiraishi, coach of Maui Swim Club, from Hawaii, and would appreciate if I could see him train. She spoke English and escorted us (my wife and four children, sister-in-law and her husband) through the tunnel and stopped at the entrance to the pool. She pointed out where Gross was swimming and gave me a chair and strict instructions not to talk to him until he was through training.

I sat about 10 feet from the edge of the pool and watched him for about two hours. During the time that I was there, he never spoke to anyone. He constantly looked at the huge clock on the wall while during his repetitions. A man I thought was his coach brought a bottle of water occasionally.

Gross towered at six feet seven inches and his arm span was so wide that he was labeled: "The Albatross."

When he finally came out of the pool, I introduced myself and said I would like to take a picture of him and his coach. He said, "No, he is not my coach. He is my assistant coach." I was stunned. His loyalty to his head coach was beyond reproach. I then asked him if it was OK to have a picture with me. He approved.

On the way out, I thanked the lady for her courtesy. While we were walking to our cars, my wife informed me that the lady at the entrance was Michael's mother. Evidently, while I was watching Michael, my wife and her sister and brother-in-law were intimately conversing.

The following morning we went back to the pool and gave Michael's mother a bunch of delicious chocolate-covered mac-nut goodies. I told her then that Coach Gambril offered Michael a full scholarship to the University of Alabama. She laughed softly, amused, and said that Michael received offers from Stanford, USC, University of California and many other colleges. However, Michael turned all of them down and said that he would rather show his loyalty to his coach and club and stay in Germany.

When we returned to Maui, I sent a photograph of Gross and me to Coach Gambril to show him that I really met Gross. To my utter surprise, Coach Gambil sent the photo back to me with Michael's signature. It so happened that, when I sent the picture, Gross was training at the University of Alabama.

Age Group Swimming Today

If Maui Swim Club was able to bring the Hawaiian Championship trophy to Maui, perhaps another local club may be able to do the same. The logical club at this time is the Lahaina Swim Club, under Tom Popdan, with membership twice the size of any club on Maui. Tom hails from Pennsylvania and is an instructor at Sacred Hearts in Lahaina.

Before the formation of the real Lahaina Swim Club, the original swimmers swam under a coach who was a faculty member of Lahainaluna. This young lady, Cheryl (Tsutsui) Seina, swam for the Hilo Swim Club on the Big Island as a child and knew me because we had home-and-home swim meets with the Hilo Swim Club several times. This original bunch of youngsters were not affiliated with any club.

After the birth of a child, the coach called and said that she did not have enough time to coach. I was asked to organize and to demonstrate the different stroke techniques and the rules governing each stroke to the newcomers.

I took Kristen Nagata, Tami Hondo, Shari Irimata, Kamuela Kanekoa and Neil Ichiki to demonstrate after our training at the Kahului Pool. I alternated taking the girls and boys on different days.

106

When the swimmers became competent to compete, they wanted to join the Maui Swim Club. I insisted several times that they should form their own Lahaina Swim Club. A person by the name of Jim Mestanza appeared. Jim was a former swimmer from the Mainland and married an attractive Canadian. He said that he would be happy to be the coach in Lahaina under the wing of Maui Swim Club.

I still insisted that Lahaina should have its own swim club. After a short spell, Jim kind of lost interest and a new-comer by the name of Christie Bussard took over. Christie was the daughter of Ray Bussard of Tennesee State, who was a member of the USA Olympic coaching staff many years ago. She had a resume and recommendations a mile long attesting to her qualifications as a coach. After our meeting, I told her that her resume was too good to coach on Maui and said that all the coaches of Maui Swim Club were strictly volunteers and were not paid. She said that it was OK with her. I felt at that time she was attempting to get a foot hold on Maui as a coach.

However, somehow, she managed to receive payment from the parents in Lahaina. About a year later, she coached the Maui Gold swimmers with hefty pay. That lasted about a year. While Christie was active during her short stint on Maui, there was a huge turn-over of swimmers going from one club to another as they followed her.

Tom Popdan arrived on the scene to form the Lahaina Swim Club. Lucky for Lahaina that Tom entered. Tom is doing an outstanding job and has been there for about 13 lucky years.

All the swimming coaches on Maui are young, energetic, enthusiastic and have blossomed from age-group swimming. They are now sharing their knowledge and skill with the youngsters. Maui will never run out of young, talented, former-successful-swimmer coaches.

Perhaps the most exciting and memorable events that took place in my career as a volunteer coach were returning the Hawaiian Age Group Swimming Championship trophy to Maui in 1991 after 50 years, watching 12-year-old Matthew Cerizo shattering 10 out of 12 Hawaiian records in a single season, witnessing Kim Takamori capturing all 12 individual events in 1991, having three former swimmers from Maui Swim Club qualify for the Olympics and enjoying the successes in their adult lives as former swimmers and Scouts. Another highlight was my participation as one of two Maui members of the

1996 Olympic Torch Relay Team in Newport, California. The other runner was David Sakugawa, a former marathoner great.

At 84 years of drooping-shoulder age, I am on top of the coaches' longevity ladder in the state and perhaps the most senior of all active coaches in the USA. My approximate 60-plus years of voluntary coaching complement my age. I have coached two generations from one household, and I sure would love to have the privilege and satisfaction of seeing the third generation come to the Kahului Pool as a member of the Maui Swim Club.

-30-

Some Pages from My Scrapbook

When my brother was in combat in Europe, he wrote home about the cold and the war conditions. Reports of casualties and men killed in combat from Maui were filtering onto the front pages of *The Maui News*. This inspired me to write the following poem. It was first published in our Maui High School newsletter, *Maui Hi-Notes*. Someone at *The Maui News* thought it was worth inserting into that newspaper , where it appeared January 26, 1944.

We'll Be Gone!

No time to say "hello" or "goodbye,"
No time for warmth or a wink,
'Cause we're training.
We're learning to kill and kill,
Not our chums, but the "devils,"
So you can live in peace.

We know this is inhuman,
But it must be done
For Victory is good.
Grand are the battles which we win,
Be they small or great, but valiant for right,
And onward to peace.

You say to us, "Win the war"
And other blood streaming phrases,
So peace will come,
We say to you back home
To win the war also,
For we can't win if you lose.

But we can't be dreaming of home now,
For we're out in the mountains and swamps
Preparing for war,
'Tis bitter cold here, but we must stay.

109

So near is God to us and our Allies
We're not afraid.

When the world is young again
And the soft earth springs forth green,
We'll be gone!
It is up to you, young friends back home
Not to make the soft earth brown again
Or our fight's in vain.

The sacrifices of my brother and the other WWII warriors allowed us to live in peace, and my Army life included swimming for my country while stationed in Europe. I received this patch as a member of the U.S. Team at the Britannia Shield Games in 1951.

Upper Paia, with the Paia Mill in the foreground. Our punawai is at the top of this photo. The road to Makawao is at left. Alexander & Baldwin Sugar Museum photo.

One of the highlights of my life was running in the Olympic Torch Relay in Newport, California, in 1996.

Made in the USA
Charleston, SC
06 March 2011